MW01535498

The Last Relationship Book You Will Ever Need
By Jeremiah Dotson

Table Of Contents

Acknowledgments

Thank you God for allowing the publication of my 13th book. Thank you to everyone who has supported my vision and passion. Thank you for all the positive comments, which have given me the drive to continue. And thank you for the negative comments, which ironically have given me the drive to continue as well. Mark and Corey, I love you.

Logic Point Number One: Relationships are about the biggest crock of shit since the thing of all men are created equal. Now all men may have been created equal but they damn sure were not and still are not viewed as such. If the thing of relationships weren't such a crock, then they all would plain and simply last. So let's cut the bullshit. The idea of a relationship is what everybody and his or her mother actually want for the relationship instead of the actual relationship and this is because the idea of all relationships is that for some strange reason or other, they all are going to be happy. The fact that everybody walking the face of this earth has his or her own interpretation of what a happy relationship entails is what makes the idea of a relationship so fucking appealing and irresistible that everybody cannot wait to jump into one. The fact that everybody walking the face of this earth has his or her own interpretation of what a happy relationship entails is also what fucks up so many people's actual happiness that not relationships, but the idea of should be against the fucking law.

Logic Point Number Two: Feelings are the most necessary and at the same time most unnecessary things in relationships. The reason why is because your feelings, what you care about, what you think is important to you or the world at large, will never be the same as the person you are involved with. To you, your feelings may be the most important thing in the world. Your partner or the one you are interested in may think or feel 'fuck your feelings.' And the funny thing about this is the fact that the 'fuck your feelings' belief is not always intentional. You see, some people are raised to be selfish. They are taught to be selfish with their money, their time and their concern. In other words they only know how to concern themselves with themselves. – It's easy to fuck and not care about the person you are fucking or to quickly forget about the person you are fucking. Trust me, people do it all the time.

Logic Point Number Three: Everybody in every relationship in existence will fuck up sooner or later. It is not a question of if but when. The reason why is because nobody knows everything about the individual he or she chooses to date or embark on a relationship with. Relationships by design are a learning experience. They are intended to be learning experiences for life, just like life itself. And I'm sure everybody will agree that everyday you learn something. The fact that far too many people are unknowingly looking for perfection when or before they get involved is what will place their relationships on the path to failure.

Chapter

1

Reasons Why Your Relationship Is A Fraud

Two of the biggest lies this wonderful world of ours has to offer, are all men are created equal and relationships are about love. Men are not created equal, babies are created equal. Once these children become men and women, that is when the separation of that equality begins. The prevailing and driving belief about relationships is that they are all based on a belief. And that belief is the one of long term happiness. The one thing that many in relationships do not immediately realize about their involvement with others and what I believe should be taught in elementary school is that the relationship you have is often based on your attractiveness. Now sure there are those who will say that guys are visual creatures and all they do is fill their vision up with the biggest asses and most proportionately sized breasts they can find but this is only true for some individuals. What is true for all individuals is the fact that everybody is a visual creature. We all look at the opposite sex. The only difference is that we look at the opposite sex for different reasons. The one thing that we as human beings have in common is that we love things of beauty. This is an indisputable fact. No one can say that they are turned on, excited or intrigued by something, which repulses them physically. Men are attracted to good looking women and women are attracted to good looking men. There is no getting around this. When people say that they are not interested in an individual's looks, either they are lying or the looks factor is not that high on the criteria list. But don't be fooled. The criteria list containing looks is still there. You see if this weren't the case, then in infidelity situations, you would not have the significant other looking average and the one who was recruited for sex being much more attractive or if not much more attractive, then not in the same class appearance wise as the significant other. You see, people will deal with others because they are average in one department but excel in others. They will deal with others, infidelity wise, because of the same reason. A man may deal with an average woman who is an excellent cook, excellent childcare provider and very adequate money earner. He may deal with somebody outside of the relationship who does not excel on any of the above except looks. Women do the same thing. Don't believe that just because a man or woman has an absolutely gorgeous significant other, that the relationship is all cookies and cream. People initiate relationships many times on what other people will think and say. An attractive significant other will many times make everyone around assume that everything in the relationship is happy and many times this is why relationships, which are no good for either party are allowed to continue. You see children are never taken to a sewage plant on a field trip and told 'look beyond the surface for the beauty.' They are taught 'that there is beauty in everything, except when there isn't.' Now there will also be those who will say things to the effect of 'I only like him or her for their personality' which in my opinion is utter bullshit. And this is because personality is something that is noticed after the initial noticing of appearance. The bottom line here is that people like you or find interest in you because you look good or you look acceptable enough for them to be seen with or you look good enough for them to stretch the initial conversation to finding out whether or not they like your personality. And if they don't, you best believe that you will never be taken around their circle of influence – aka friends and family. Now once you get past the looks, you will have to examine why it is you are interesting to the other party. Many people will be under the impression that because they find themselves smart or intelligent or whatever else, that the one who is interested in them will find them interesting for the same reasons. Not always. Deception is one of man's greatest weapons. Keep saying that to yourselves because when people believe the opposite and start believing that everybody in this world who shows interest in you is just as good as you, heartbreak and hurt is imminent. Going back to the above for a second, when you put your best foot forward and look absolutely outstanding and people start to approach you with a relationship as the goal, you should automatically be on the defensive. Reason being: if they approach you for how you look, they are not really concerning themselves with what else you have to offer. Which is why I always advise people who are in search of a relationship, to walk around looking presentable but average. You see, some people will actually spend over an hour getting themselves ready to make a twenty minute trip to the store. Doesn't make too much sense, now does it? And the reason that many of these individuals will give for taking so long to get ready, when you will only be out for a short period of time is 'you never know who you might meet.' Now this is true, you can never tell whom you may run into, but my thing is this: whomever you run into, wouldn't you want them to like or respect you based on you and not the false persona you present? Here's the thing: when you always look good, people will always expect you to always look good. And the one or few times that you don't, people will think that its impossible that you did, or they will think something must be really wrong for you to do so. It's the same with relationships.

People always expect that because they see no unhappiness or adversity, that there never is or never will be any adversity – and then when there is, people are thrown into such a state of disbelief that sometimes they cannot put back together the idea that maybe you were just being normal. You see, what more people need to do is embody the laundry day appearance to weed out those individuals who have that one aspect relationship mentality. When you look average, you will not stand out based on attractiveness alone. You will not have people exclaiming 'Damn! Look at that ass! Or 'OMG! He looks like a movie star!' You will coerce others to judge and accept you based on intelligence or actual personality or one of many other factors besides the way your body is proportioned or how pretty or handsome your face happens to be. I mean people should already know this but if the opposite sex approaches you and sex is in the first or first few conversations you have, it should not take the intelligence of a rocket scientist for you to know that this individual is not long term relationship material. Unfortunately the way society is, this foul mouth ed ness is not frowned upon. It is welcomed. A man can say 'damn ma, let me lay in that for a little while' (and I have actually heard this from one complete stranger to another) and the woman will smile and respond with something to the effect of 'you so crazy!' Many women will act the same way toward men so please don't think I am picking only on the men here but the point, which is trying to be made here is that these people who accept those who are about as far away from couth and sophistication as could be, also expect those to be able to change at the drop of a hat and become relationship material exactly when the other wants them to. Here's a bit of relationship advice, if the way the person you are interested in, acts toward you is not good for everybody else, then you should not be allowing or accepting the way that person acts with you in the first place. But see the problem with some people is that they have no respect for themselves – or they have the type of respect, which is selective. In other words, one day they have it and the next day they don't. In regard to relationships, it should be a thing of you talk to me with respect and you talk to others with the same type of respect because here's the thing: if a man for example, like the one above said to you hey ma, can I lay in that for a little while? Which is the equivalent of Miss, can I fuck you for a little while? How happy would you as a woman be, if that question was asked of someone else, especially if the two of you were in a relationship? I'm guessing not one fucking bit. So my question is why do certain women, matter of fact, why do people accept things like this at all? Now true, nobody can control anybody's actions but an individual's actions while around you are what will always give insight to how they will act in regard to the rest of their life when they are not with you. The reason or main reason why someone will dress too fashionably or too revealing is because they have little else to offer in regard to a relationship. They will go out and try to attract a man or woman instead of leaving it up to chance and fate and all that other good stuff. The fact that they are rushing their opportunities is a clear cut sign that they are somehow deficient in their thinking or existence. It is always a good thing to be presentable. However, when you feel the need to spend a weekly paycheck on one outfit or on one pair of shoes or apply the amount of makeup, which if removed, will make you look totally different, that is a cry for help. It is a show of desperation. This is what people see and this is what makes people treat you a certain way. They will either run from you or approach you with less than honorable intentions. The problem that people have is that they rush. Instead of waiting for what is destined to come, they attempt to rush fate and destiny. They say I want this type of individual or any individual for that matter and I will dress or act a certain way to catch this individual instead of dressing like I normally do and acting like myself and waiting for the individual who is supposed to come into my life, to do so. This is society's problem. Everything has to be fast. Everything has to be what's popular. Nobody wants to trust and believe in a higher power to send them somebody who is good for them instead of somebody who will make them happy for a quick fix. Too many people want to believe that they have control of their lives. They want to believe that nothing happens by chance – or if it does, then they had a hand in making it happen. This is another reason why so many relationships fail. Relationships are different than everything else in life in the respect that you cannot just go and get one, like say a job. Now a relationship is like a job – but AFTER you get it. A relationship is something you have to wait for, rather the right relationship is something you have to wait for. You wait for a job and that shit may never come. You have to go and get a job. You have to go and get a place to live. You have to basically do everything in life in this manner but a relationship, it will come. When you force a relationship, by dressing a certain way, acting a certain way and just being uncharacteristically who you are not, your relationship, if you ever do achieve one, will be based on a lie. And as such, will grow from that foundation of lying. And in case any of you are unaware of this, a lie will never grow into the truth. People who start relationships on lies will have to keep living those lies all throughout the relationship to keep the same level of interest as when the relationship was initiated. That's entirely too much work. People should be always be themselves so that there will be one less thing to worry about as the relationship progresses. You see if people cannot like you for who you are, then these are not people that you want to have a relationship with anyway. Unless it's just sexual. (ijs)

Now the first and most controversial reason why your relationship is more than likely a fraud is that you and your partner will do anything to ensure each other's happiness – within reason of course. Now I know many of you are probably saying doing anything and everything in a relationship for the other party is what is supposed to be done, so how could this activity be fraudulent? Here's the thing: the word anything, is a word and thought process which, includes lying. The unfortunate hypocrisy about this is that there is no room for deception in a positive and progressive relationship but deception is necessary for the relationship to continue. One of the first things people do when weighing the options for a relationship is decide amongst themselves how much deception they will either indulge in or allow themselves to be a part of. And this deception is perpetrated by people accepting things, which they know they do not initially like but will accept because they either have intentions on changing the behavior or not remaining in the relationship for long enough for the behavior to have a major effect on them. People for example, accept those who smoke even though they don't and even though they find the practice disgusting. They deal with these people on a relationship level because these people have something that the other wants. That something could be that the other is very attractive. The other is a solidified slut in the bedroom or things of that nature. There is something, which makes the first forego common sense and acceptance to deal with something he or she does not like. In addition to this, they feel in their hearts that eventually they will be able to get the other to change his or her behavior.

The second thing, which is proof that the relationship is deceit laced, is the myth of total and complete honesty to the significant other. Now I have said this on countless occasions but people still doubt the validity of this statement. Nobody in a relationship is always honest about everything, which goes on in his or her relationship, all of the time. There is deception somewhere. Now the deception could be straight up or it could be the deception by omission thing but there will be deception nonetheless. Proof of this is how nobody in his or her right mind will tell the significant other about dreams he or she may have of the sister or brother of the significant other but this happens all the time. A woman will get involved with one brother based on how well the other brother treats his wife and family. She will do so on the hopes that this brother will be the same and do the same for her. The same thing happens with a man getting involved with certain women. If the girl of his dreams is already married or involved, he may involved himself with the sister of this woman because in his mind he will believe that everything she does for her significant other will be the same things that the sister will do for him. And this belief will be because since they are cut from the same cloth, they will more than likely do the same things. But you see, this is one of the things that people will never tell to the significant other. And more times than not, it doesn't seem to work out that way. For a less disheartening example, and on the side of straight up deception, there is the weight issue. Many will not truthfully answer the question of am I getting fat, when the answer is yes. They will give one of those relationship helping, white lies, so that the significant other will not feel unattractive to society at large, themselves and most importantly, the significant other. You see, a person who is repulsed by a fat person will not say I hate you because you are fat, he or she will more than likely act distant, act different or act in a manner, which is not conducive to the long term happiness of the relationship. And since nine times out of ten, the person who may not like the fact that the other is a little bigger than what he or she usually prefers, needs something from the relationship that the other provides, he or she will act the part of somebody who is not bothered by the weight gain at all. One reason this type of deception happens is because the significant other looks so good when the relationship is initiated and the 'look so good' significant other is one who feels that he or she will always look so good and doesn't need to do daily or weekly upkeep, say for instance like going to a gym. This person may even be one of those highly hopeful and disillusioned individuals, who believe that love should be based on the inside of an individual and not the outward appearance. Yeah, maybe if this were a perfect world. This is what needs to be learned and remembered; many people base relationships on three things: one, how good you look, two, what you can do for me, and three, what you can do for me. Relationships are not based on 'I can make his life so much better or I can make her life so much better.' They are selfish in nature. They are 'damn she looks good, everybody will be impressed when I show up at the family reunion with her on my arm.' They are 'damn he looks good, he will definitely give me a pretty baby!' They are 'this person has money. He or she can take care of me and my family.' Has anybody ever seen or heard of a relationship being initiated on the opposite? Of course not. You see one of the things relationships are based on, is the hope of future happiness. They are continued through trial and error. The hope is always positive. The continuation, not so much.

Another reason relationships are fraudulent, along with anticipation, is the sometimes overwhelming expectation. People expect that there will always be calls about nothing, three to four times a day. They expect that everything, which was done by members of their circle of influence for their husbands and wives, will be done by their significant other for them. They even expect that every time they are thinking about the significant other, the significant other will be thinking about them but this is not always the case. Deception plays a bigger part in most relationships than many people know and a bigger part in relationships that many people want to accept. You see when it comes to deception, people will anticipate the expectations of the other and they will act accordingly. They will say things like 'he or she will expect me to do this, so I will do it only because of the fact that they expect me to do it, and not because I want to or should do it.' You see, people are taught deception from the time they are young. And they are many times taught this from those who are supposed to be teaching them everything except that deception. Parents are telling girls in not so many words use your vagina to get a man. Not love, not intellect, but your vagina. Once you get a man he will take care of you forever so you never have to use your brain or anything besides the vagina. Young ladies grow up believing this and when the relationship ends due to death of the primary caretaker or divorce or separation, the women have nowhere to turn. The real bad thing about what this deception leads to is that when these women who have no marketable skills or no redeeming qualities other than the ability to accurately handle a male organ are left without support, they stick out like a sore thumb in the grand scheme of those looking for relationships. Now what is even worse about this scenario is that certain men will gravitate towards these women for no reason other than the fact that they are in need. Now it should be stated that everybody is in need of something when they go looking for a relationship. The only difference is that the needs of these women primarily revolve around money. So what do some men do? They flaunt exactly what it is they think the women are in need of. And those who are in need will make a beeline for those men like a fish will blindly chase after a worm on a hook. We all know what happens then. The women who use their vaginas continue to do so thinking that the vagina will keep the man. The man will use the vagina of this one and that one and of every woman who was taught the deception explained above. Then what happens is the belief is continued that all men ain't shit. The next belief, which is continued, is the one of the only thing women desire is money or a man to take care of them. And finally, if men and women do not fit into the type of deception explained above, they will be stereotyped into the classifications of religious, gay and or lesbian or 'they think they are too good.'

When it comes to relationships, many will say and agree that they have a certain level of deception in them all. I believe it goes much deeper than that. I believe relationships are rooted in bullshit. They are based on the fairy tale idea of happily ever after. Don't believe me? When was the last time you heard any relationship story end with the princess nagging the shit out of the prince for all eternity or the prince fucking every pauper he could find? You haven't. And you won't. Yet in the real world, scenarios like those described above happen all the time. Nobody is ever going to tell you when you get into a relationship that it has about a 50% chance of failure because those are some pretty high fucking odds and people want you to believe that your relationship actually has a chance at succeeding. They don't want to tell you things like the motherfucker or bitch you are dealing with may actually try and kill you in your sleep and not because he or she has caught you doing something wrong but because he or she <u>thinks</u> that you are doing something wrong. Here's more bullshit: when parents argue in the household, what is one of the first things said? 'Let's not argue in front of the children.' My question is why? Will an argument or two completely screw up the child's interpretation of love and what a happy relationship is supposed to be? Or will the avoidance of seeing ma and pa go at it every once in a while, further the bullshit belief that a happy relationship is one where you never become upset with your significant other? They both sound like bullshit to me. The problem with this world and parenting is that these good intentions will send people straight to hell. You never use profanity around your children in the hopes that they will never learn it, then they go to school and they are immersed in it. You teach your kids not to argue, then they learn the lesson they should never become upset with the significant other. The problem with these lessons is that when reality sets in, they will get the shit shocked out of them when they get into the workplace and everybody curses and they feel like the oddball. They will feel as though they married the wrong man or woman when they realize the relationship they witnessed their mother and father having is the complete opposite of the one they now have. Avoidance of adversity is never a good thing. How you handle that adversity is. How you explain to the kids why you had the argument or how you explain that some people will use a little profanity here and there and some people will curse like there are no other words in the English alphabet, is what will make for a better existence. The problem, which unwittingly kills many happy lives and relationships is the thinking of if I don't say or do this, then they will never learn or do this.

Relationships are also fraudulent because they are many times based on the historical representation of you, not because they like you. If people are into the hip hop culture for instance, they might try and become involved with someone who is a minority just because of that fact. They will many times associate the being a minority with being a part of the hip hop culture. Some people will date or involve themselves in relationships with non minorities because of the history and perception of them having money. And see, this is many times why relationships do not always work out. When you date somebody based on how you think they are going to be, instead of how they actually are, you are setting yourself up for failure in that relationship. You see, as an unwritten rule, a person should like the individual he or she is pursuing. But this world is compartmentalized into classifications. The way society is now, it is a crime, a sin, an absolute shame even, if you like somebody just because. It is twice as bad if you like somebody outside of your race 'just because' and this is again thanks to society.

Keeping The Significant Other vs. Keeping Them Happy

Okay, let's start this section by slaughtering a couple of highly publicized and much believed myths. The first myth is about longevity. People have for the longest time been under the mistaken impression that the longer a couple remains together or the longer an individual remains in a relationship, the more happiness there is in that relationship. And people reason that if you were not happy in the relationship, the relationship would not have been allowed to continue. You know the ole 'if you don't like something, then leave' thing. But this belief goes to show two things. The first is that they often project their understanding and interpretation of how things should go onto others, meaning my logic should be your logic. And the second thing is that deception is much stronger and prevalent than many people in this world realize. What should be understood is that people are mentally flexible creatures. They can adjust to any environment and be happy or comfortable in it, or they can be miserable in it but still somehow handle that situation or environment. People in jail do it all the time. This does not mean that you completely like a situation. It means that you have to deal with a situation until your circumstances improve enough to allow for the removal of that situation or circumstance. People stay with their significant others sometimes for years and this is not because of love but most often because of necessity. People have children for example and they know that the significant other has no fucking common sense, so they stay to make sure that the child or children are being well taken care of. Another example: people are undocumented. They are living in this country illegally and the significant other takes care of them but makes their life a living hell in the process. And here's one more popular example: people do not have any education, which will allow them to work and make enough money to move out on their own. Now all of these examples are many times overlooked by society at large. And not only that, these unseen examples are what's used to force others into staying in a relationship that they do not belong in. You see people on the outside will say things to the effect of you've been together so long, why don't you stay? Or why do you want to leave, you make such a good couple and other related nonsense such as that. They say these things because they do not know what goes on behind the happy, smiling faces. These people are what you can call kept but not kept happy. People who fall under the category of kept, allow themselves to get into and remain in an uncomfortable comfort zone. In other words, they are not happy but they are comfortable with what they are receiving in exchange for not receiving happiness. A popular example of this is 'I don't like this individual but they cook, provide me with sex, and give me money, so why would I leave? I'll cheat but I won't leave.' Now to keep the average individual, all someone needs to do is everything that that average individual may seem to want. 'I want a car.' 'Okay, I'll buy it for you.' 'I need some money. Okay, I'll give it to you.' 'I need sex. Okay, come here and get all you want.' Here's the million dollar question: will anybody in his or her right mind leave someone who is doing everything for them? Of course not. This is the epitome of why buy the cow when you can get the milk for free. I mean isn't the basic objective in life to get as much as you can in the time you are given? And if there is somebody who will help you with that task, wouldn't that be considered hitting the jackpot? Of course it would. In relationships, this should be the textbook ultimate goal. You help me get everything I want and I help you get everything you want and the world as we know it will be wonderful. The only thing is that there is an ironic hypocrisy surrounding this type of thinking which states that if I do everything for you, then I will not be desirable enough for you to want to pursue a relationship with me. You see, to keep somebody, all you have to do is everything they want but to keep them happy, you have to ration out your kindness. Is it just me or does that sound a tad bit retarded? You see, many people are taught that they have to get all they can. This is what leads some people to take advantage of others. Some people are aware of this and use that knowledge to classify others who do everything they say a weak, easy and presenting no challenge. They will even label these individuals as predictable. The reason these labels are thrust upon the more than willing to do whatever significant other is because certain people need their activities monitored and restricted as if they are children. People will say things like I cannot deal with you because you let me walk all over you. You let me have whatever I want and I will take advantage of that so I need somebody to tell me no. Now this knowledge of self is good, but what it does is show that the individual who says these things is not ready for a relationship. What this individual is saying is I need someone to control me and my behavior. And this is not what a relationship is supposed to be. To keep somebody happy, all that needs to be done is the allowing of them to continue to do what makes them happy. Relationships are feared because they are historically known for changing an individual into what the significant other wants. And this is not a small change, as what I believe all relationships should go through but a life changing adjustment, which will make the individual more like the significant other and less like himself. So many people don't realize that the perfect relationship is one where you can be yourself and I can be myself – together, and without infringing on each other's happiness and ability to do so. People are so much into this good girl, bad boy thing, which eventually transgresses into good girl who has turned bad boy into good boy that it is expected behavior in relationships. People do not expect girls to be bad. They do not expect bad boys who get into relationships with good girls to stay bad either. What is not realized is that you cannot keep somebody happy while forcing them to change.

Why people get involved in relationships but won't commit

The most under realized fact about life is that people in this world, will only find interest in you for three reasons: the first is companionship. The second is because you have something they want. And the third is because you have something they need. Now to understand this, the first thing people need to do is get away from this whole thing of you not allowing yourself to be used and you want 50/50 this or 50/50 that. That's bullshit. Everybody you know, or will ever know is in a relationship to use the individual he or she is in a relationship with in some manner. So let's stop all the bullshit crying about 'he used me' or 'she used me.' Of course they fucking did. If you were not usable, you would not have anything to offer and thereby would not be involved in any type of relationship. Now the want or need could be genuine or it could be deceptive. Finding out is completely up to you, not up to your significant other to tell you but up to you. And the reason why is because people for some reason or other have this belief that the significant other should never be completely aware of everything, which goes on in the mind or the past of the one they are involved with. Many times it is a trust factor. Many times it is one of deception. You see so many people do not trust the ones they involve themselves with that they will never tell the other why they need them. They figure if they tell the truth, it will somehow scare

31

the other away. The unfortunate hypocrisy is that since truth is so closely related to deception, many people will believe that you are lying when the truth is being told. Now people will commit to the significant other by their physical presence alone. They will do everything, which is done by a loving and deeply committed couple or happily married couple – but they will not commit to the significant other in their minds. Their hearts will be their own or they will belong to someone else. And this is why it is so easy for individuals to walk away without any adverse feelings when the relationship goes through adversity. The problem with this is that you will never know when you have an individual's heart, mind or body. To be in love I believe you need all three. People can speak the words of love, but they can be nothing but deception. People can mimic the actions of love but they too can be deception. People can even have sex and make it so good that you will have no choice but to believe that you are in love but again, it could be nothing but deception.

In regard to why the opposite sex won't commit, the short answer is they don't have to. And you, yes you are the culprit. You see, as stupid (and I really hate to use that word) as many of us show ourselves to be, we are unbelievably intelligent. We learn things immediately. If for example you step on somebody's foot, the response, which is given, will teach you whether it's acceptable to do it again. If you do something that makes somebody unhappy and they tell you in an effort to put a stop to it, then you know they do not like it and they will therefore not do it again, which will allow you to be happy. If you do something they like, but it causes detriment to you, if you do not inform them of your dislike in doing whatever it is, the assumption will be made that you must be enjoying it as well. And the most popular example of this is the giving the milk without having to purchase the cow thing. People will carry on engagements forever because they make the one detrimental mistake, which sends them on the road to not getting married. And that mistake is giving them married things when you are single. These married things are not always about sex. What they mainly include is the level of comfort, which drive the individual's thinking into believing that life cannot get any better. This level of comfort will make the non married individual feel that there will be no difference after the papers are signed and the vows are read, which will consequently lead the non married individual to desire to remain in the comfort level he or she has become accustomed to. And the next thing you know, somebody is never getting married but always wondering why. You see some people do not ever want to get married but they do want to be in relationships. They, for some reason or other feel that marriage is the great definitive as far as being able to keep their options open.

So what they will many times do is what I like to call give 65% toward the relationship. This means that just like in school, where a grade of 65% is passing, these people will do just enough to sustain the relationship. They will do everything except get married and this is because the influence of society, along with the knowledge of everything that this particular individual has done for the relationship, will make the other think 'well since he or she has done this much, I will be a selfish fool if I let him or her go just because I wanted to get married. And see this is how people stay single forever. One can take care of the kids. He or she can pay bills and take the other out whenever requested. He or she can be there for emergencies and for related times of support. Basically this individual can do everything except marry the other and he or she will do everything so well and so much that the other will eventually downgrade the importance of the marriage thing to little more than a piece of paper.

Now with the example above, a person can give another things, which are only supposed to be done in a marriage capacity before the marriage is underway. And both may enjoy the things, which are given. If one has other intentions, such as eventually getting married, then this individual cannot reasonably think that the other will indulge in a marriage to continue getting the single benefit. Consequently, this individual cannot rescind the things, which were being given as a way of forcing the other to indulge in the marriage because nine times out of ten, the marriage will be based on little more than what was being given in order for them to get married. People do things, which the other will many times mistakenly interpret as only being done because the other loves them. When people for whatever reason stop doing these things, the thought will be that the other does not love him or her like they used to.

People won't commit for a variety of reasons. The main reason is they don't like you in a commitment capacity. Now what this means is they like you initially. They want to fuck you. They may even take you around a few of their friends but that is about the extent of their like. And the thing about this type of like, is the fact that it can go on throughout the entire relationship. You see relationships are supposed to be about progression. Supposed to be. However some people can remain in the 'phase one' arena for the duration of the relationship. And this is because people need instruction regarding 'your' life. Yes, everybody needs instruction on what to do to make their own lives better but a relationship is about two people. If they are happy because they have all the instruction they need to make their lives better and don't know what you need, either because you did not tell them or because they did not care to ask, guess what? You won't be happy. If you want progression from the relationship, you have to tell them that you want to get married and not in the way that all too many dead end relationships go where an individual will say 'I want to get married eventually.' No, you have to put a stipulation on the relationship that you are comfortable with losing. If you are comfortable investing a year of your life then that is the stipulation. If you are comfortable with investing ten years to see if this person a) wants to get married and b) is marriage material, then that is your stipulation. But don't make the mistake of waiting until you get fed up from not getting proposed to or until somebody else who you have the same level of interest in as you had from your significant other when you two first got together approaches, and then try to force on him or her an ultimatum. And please don't make the mistake of using anyone else's stated or suggested time of investment as your own. It may take them one year to know if a person is the right fit but it may take you five. Neither of you are any more right than the other. You have to say that you want to have kids and so on and so forth. You see too many relationships are they like you, you like them, you start fucking and you keep fucking. And that's it. This is why relationships fail. A plan has to be put in place for how you want and expect your lives together to turn out and the two of you must be in agreement with the plan otherwise you will be stuck in that phase one arena. Now be aware that there is a fine line of difference between making a plan as far as how you want and expect your life and relationship to turn out and coercing somebody else to do what it is they don't want to do but will do so as to make you happy. You see forcing anybody in this world to do something they don't like or prefer not to do falls under the umbrella of unhappiness or discontent. The main unwritten rule in any relationship is to hurt the significant other as little as possible. Unhappiness is often indistinguishable from hurt. You see in a perfect world people could be completely honest with their feelings and intentions and the other party in the relationship would be mature enough and stable enough to handle them. However this is not a perfect world and many times people's feelings and apprehensions are what dictate if and how a relationship will go. If people hurt the one they are interested in the interest will usually not go any further. This is why people lie. This is why people prolong things, which should not be allowed to go on and this is why many relationships are frauds.

Some people have this belief that marriage or exclusivity is not for them or feel that it is only for certain people. And this is what others have to realize they are fighting against. Some people feel that because the one they are interested in does not want to get married then something is wrong with them that makes them unable to become married. People have many different levels of criteria on what makes somebody marriage material. Sometimes they divulge this to others and sometimes not. The hard part about relationships is that you have to sometimes drag it out of the one you are interested in. And this is because often they won't tell you so that they can keep getting what it is they need from you, and as stated above, you will unfortunately be in that phase one, no progression stage for the rest of your life.

People get into for relationships for many reasons. The stay in relationships for many reasons. Nine times out of ten, the reasons, which cause them to get into the relationships, are completely different than the reasons, which cause them to stay committed. A lot of people have ideas on what they want from the significant other. These ideas are more commonly called incorrect thought processes. These people figure he or she will cook every night, take care of the kids, keep a clean house and have a stable religious foundation on which to build. But yet these people go and try to find all of these attributes and more in the first person they see, at the first club or party or bar they go to. Now I am not saying that it is impossible to find a good man or woman at a place historically known for not having good men or women, but it should be known how individuals act before they get involved in relationships is often a good indicator of how they will continue to act after they get involved in relationships. I hear all the time people, yes, men and women, saying they met somebody at the bar, hooked up and now want to pursue a relationship with that person. Here's the thing: <u>Many</u> of the people who hang out in bars and clubs and party much of the time are not marriage material. They are bar and club material. Now this is not to say that they are bad people. No. They are many times not the types of individuals who fit into the stay at home, cook dinner every night and take care of the kids in a responsible manner kind of classification. <u>All</u> of the people, who have sex or perform sex acts with you upon first meeting, are not in the correct frame of mind to be able to enter into a long term relationship. You see people do not frequent these types of establishments trying to find a husband or wife. They go trying to have fun. Marriages or long term relationships cannot be based on or initiated on fun and this is because they will fail or they will not be happy.

Another reason people won't commit is aside from the above, they feel that you have put them into a different classification of priority. In other words they do not feel as important as you may have made them once feel. This is accomplished by many things. One of those is as simple as them calling and you not picking up but calling back half an hour later without any explanation why. Or if there is an explanation, it is the famous 'I'll tell you about it later' and we all know what happens then, later never comes. Now the reason for this could be absolutely nothing derogatory. The one in question could be shopping and forget. He or she could just say I don't feel like talking and refuse to pick up the phone. Any reason at all could be why but the thing, which will cause suspicion, is that the reasons were not divulged and explained. Yes some people are needy like that where they need to know every move of the significant other – and if they don't, they will feel that the significant other is not being completely truthful and will cause the significant other to be placed into a position of no longer long term material. Some people, if they live apart, will do things like get up and go about their day, doing whatever it is they have to do, while not contacting the other till the day is damn near done. This will make the other feel like he or she is not as important as what ever it is the first had to do. Now granted, the other could have as easily called to find out what's up with the other but people have this perpetual expectation of 'if I don't call you, then you should call me. I should not always be calling you and you should not always be calling me.' I tell people this all the time; it is not the big things in relationships, which cause their demise but the small, overlooked ones. Now we all should know that in regard to the above, it is little more than a trust issue. The one does not trust himself or herself and he or she projects the distrust onto the significant other. Sometimes people have been hurt so bad in relationships, that they need to be constantly reassured that the other is not doing anything dirty, otherwise they will feel that the other is, even if he or she has given no reason to believe so. The real big problem with this is the fact that more times than not, the significant other who is committing these infractions will downplay the importance of these infractions. They will feel that they are nothing for the significant other to worry about. Many times the significant other, whose concerns are being trivialized, will leave the relationship. In other words, if I don't feel I am important to you or this relationship, why am I here?

What should never be forgotten when it comes to relationships is that they are ALWAYS about necessity. Think about it, when women portray themselves, as having only one thing to offer, as what many of these scantily clad and overly obnoxious women seem to do, many men will deem that they have but only one form of usefulness. And that one form of usefulness is what we all know as being a sperm receptacle. You see people have to understand that no matter how much Hollywood and the reality shows make loud, aggressive, whore like women appealing, the grim reality is that men do not really desire these women for the long term. You see once you outlive your usefulness; your presence is not really warranted. In other words once they get through using you, whether that use is sexually or financially, you will be discarded. If you are not discarded physically, then you will be discarded emotionally. In other words the individual you are with will stop caring about you or anything you do and while you are sitting there wondering why the significant other is becoming distant, the significant other is either screwing or thinking about screwing the next chick who can provide the next level of usefulness. Men are used in the same manner at times also; only difference is people don't talk about it. Some women see a man and think there goes a handsome dick - in other words a sperm bank. In other words all I want from you is your semen. And then so many people wonder why after a child is conceived or delivered, the relationship goes to shit. You see this whole deception thing occurs on both sides of the spectrum. Men use women for things and women use men for things. What this world has a ginormous problem of believing is 'no, he wouldn't do that' or no, she wouldn't do that.' Newsflash, PEOPLE WILL DO ANYTHING IN THIS WORLD. Just in case you have never watched the news, people are in jail because they do harm to the significant others for making them believe that they are the parent of one, two or six kids, none of whom may actually be theirs. People get pregnant and take the fuck off, zoom, bye, bye. Never to be seen again. People have babies and steal the babies from the comfortable environment they are used to, from the mommy or daddy the child is getting used to, from the loving extended family that the child may so desperately need, all because the child is all they wanted in the first place.

Why Relationships Continue To Fail

In my opinion, one of the most profound sayings in this world, is the one that goes 'those who do not learn from the mistakes of the past are doomed to repeat them.' The reason I believe this saying to be so profound is because it is one of the truest things, which can be said. This is true for life in general and especially true for relationships. In regard to relationships, one of the oldest reasons for failure is still one of the most prevalent. And that is the basic rule of communicating effectively to the significant other. You have to talk to the person you are in the relationship with. This part, I know all of you know. But the part you might not know is how. There are two different types of talking and I am not referring to the verbal / non verbal thing. I am speaking of the general, generic conversations and the what really bothers you about the significant other. Now aside from everything else mentioned in this publication, from lack of respect, all the way to lack of trust, the most basic form of unhappiness still seems to be that of not being able to talk to the one you are involved with in a relationship. Now here's the strange thing about non communication: when in a relationship, people can still have sex, without communication. People can still have get togethers with friends and family, without communication. People can still even raise their kids in the same household and not have that decent, necessary communication. But the bottom line is that with all a couple can and will have, minus the above stated things and more, the one thing, which is guaranteed to be missing is being happy. Too many relationships fail because of the initial deception perpetrated to get into the relationship. The ole long term venture with the short term mindset thing is definitely a factor. What people do is either have it in their minds that the relationship they get into is going to last forever or until one of them dies – or the relationship they get into is going to last until it doesn't period. Not both. The problem, all too often is that people with these two opposing thought processes continue to become involved with one another and continue to wonder why their relationships have problems or fail. You see, the one simple thing that individuals in relationships have to do to keep the relationship going is to work together to keep it going. When one person works to keep it going and the other is just like whatever, the relationship may last but there will be a great amount of strain on one party. This is the equivalent of a tug of war. Both parties are pulling in the opposite direction and we all know what's eventually going to happen. One will lose. Many in relationships do not understand this. What they do is say 'he or she doesn't talk to me anymore, they just sit around and watch tv or stay to themselves.' And the other accepts this. That's the crazy part. When the relationship began, almost nobody sat around disrespecting the significant other. Nobody walked around the house not speaking to or interacting with the significant other but magically and mysteriously, the relationship has reached a point where it is perfectly okay. Does anybody else see something wrong with this equation? A relationship, as we all know or should know, is a <u>continuous effort.</u> The very minute, the very second in fact, when one of the parties in the relationship stops working toward making the relationship happy, the other should stop and attempt to figure out why. You see, you can't just say 'oh he or she will get over whatever is going on in their life' and this is because sometimes he or she may not. He or she may be miserable and you could, rather should be the one thing to pull them out of that pit of misery. If you don't, the significant other could very well be miserable for the rest of his or her life. And number one, they could blame you for not helping them out of their despair, and two, you could develop such a resistance to it that you could become comfortable not speaking to or interacting with the other for years. When people in relationships say 'I don't feel like being bothered' you have to be the one to take the stance and say 'I'm not going to let you feel like not being bothered. It is my job to bother you.' That's what a relationship is. If they ever get to a point where they can honestly say they don't want you to help them with whatever it is they are going through, then the point has been reached when they no longer value you. You should then ask yourself, if the person you have given your life to, does not need you, why are you in his or her life? What almost everybody in a relationship knows but conveniently forgets every so often is that a relationship is so much more than the physical act of being in a relationship. Many more people don't understand this. These people confuse the longevity aspect with the love aspect and feel that the longer you are with somebody, the more you love and care for this person. And sometimes people outside of a relationship will use that incorrect knowledge to pressure those in the relationship to stay together. They use their twisted reasoning to say things like you've been together this long, why would you want to leave? Some people feel that because they are in a relationship with somebody and they say 'you know what, fuck you its over!' That it is actually over in the mind of the significant other. This is how you have those misunderstood situations of infidelity. This is how you have one person saying its over, then going out and trying to find a new relationship while the other is sitting at home mad thinking that the other is sitting home mad too and just needs time to cool off. A relationship is a work in progress. It is a continuing effort. It is the journey, not the destination. The confusing thing about relationships is that an individual in a relationship may stop the journey, may stop working on progression, may stop the continuing effort but still remain in the relationship. This is confusing because the people who observe this will more than likely never know. And this extends from the significant other to those outside the relationship.

Another reason relationships will continue to fail is because people in them never live up to the expectations of the other. Now everybody knows that there are and will be expectations but meeting those sometimes beyond astronomical pieces of criteria, are one of the things keeping many people lonely. People have expectations, which go from one end of the life spectrum to the other. They have expectations regarding sex, as in we have to do it this many times a day and this many times a week, all the way to when we do it, the performance must be on the level of this porn star or that porn star. People have expectations regarding children and the appropriate way they should be raised by both parents, from dads should be doing manly things like playing sports and teaching the male children how to fix the car, to women having the expectation that they should be doing only woman things, like teaching the female children how to cook, clean and basically be subservient to or take care of the man. There are even expectations regarding finances and this seems to be one of the biggest detriment causing issues in relationships today. You see, many people are under the impression that not couples supporting each other, but men supporting the women financially, is the main expectation in a relationship. This expectation has gotten so out of hand that relationships are initiated many times on that fact alone and not only that, relationships are ended because people are not able to meet the expectation, which was set forth many times before the relationship was even initiated. This point cannot be stated enough: people already have an idea of what the significant other is supposed to do, be and accomplish in his or her life, and within the relationship, even before the relationship is underway. The problem with this expectation is that more times than not, the people with these expectations will never relay that information to the significant other. In addition to individuals not relaying the message of what they want, need and expect from the significant other, the big problem is that these individuals will never help the significant other achieve what the other is lacking. If the significant other has a less than lucrative job, the other will leave instead of encouraging the other to go back to school and better his or her financial situation. The other will ridicule and berate the first on what little money is made as opposed to helping the first get a better or second source of income. If it is a sex thing, people nine times out of ten will not even discuss that. They will more than likely continue to pretend that they are enjoying the act until something better comes along. And as we all know, this is mainly done for the other benefits the relationship provides. The other big problem with the relationship expectation is that besides it being all gender related, it is most of the time wrong. Too many women are out here thinking that all a man wants to do is play video games, watch sports and fuck. And too many men are out here thinking that all women want to do is look pretty, take money from men and fuck. You see, this thinking will unfairly compartmentalize people into categories, which they may never escape. And because of the type of classification they are placed into, they may never be respected or thought of as being able to do anything else. This is why women talk to women about certain things and vice versa. You see if people, both men and women thought and actually believed that relationships were not just for as long as they are going good, but forever, then they would get to know everything there is to know about the one they are involved with. But see, people don't do this. People do not trust the ones they are involved in a relationship with. They do not give them the respect for being able to understand everything that they may be going through. They do not feel comfortable enough to divulge everything they have experienced in their lives – but yet and still they wanna become involved in relationships. You see, this is part of the deception that people in relationships perpetrate against one another all the time. Now what should be understood is that there will be some things that people will never be comfortable talking about. The way this fucked up world is, so many people suffer traumatic experiences and abuses from the time they are very young and many of these people do not have the proper outlet to discuss or release the memories or feelings surrounding the event. These people could carry the pain around within themselves for years and suppress it so well that no one would ever even think to ask. But you see, no matter how well certain experiences are suppressed, they will resurface in one form or other and cause some type of detriment in the relationship. You see many times people will get involved with these people and think that the other is just crazy but they will have no idea where their interpretation of crazy stems from. They will just focus on how an individual may be acting at the time and respond accordingly. In regard to the above, If every man said and thought I want one woman to give every aspect of my existence to from the time I meet her, until the time I die, and every woman did the same, there would never be an instance of infidelity again. But as stated above, far too often the people in relationships do not trust one another. Hell, many times they do not even trust themselves. In my opinion a relationship is 50% getting to know somebody as completely as you can. And the other 50% is allowing them to do the same.

Another common reason relationships fail is because people are not taught how to handle the level of unhappiness they experience in a productive manner. For instance, some people will experience an extreme level of adversity or extreme in their mind, and over react, say to the point of throwing the significant other out of the home. And this is done not because the significant other desires for the relationship to be over but because the significant other desires that oh so elusive peace of mind. The significant other wants for whatever unhappiness he or she is experiencing to stop – quickly. The most common way for this to happen is for them to be separated. The bad thing about this is that sooner or later the significant other is going to calm down. He or she is going to regret the decision, which was made to evict the other from his or her place of residence. The real bad thing about this is that while one has flung the significant other out of the house, that significant other is thinking or feeling that he or she has flung him or her out of their life – and not only that, he or she will begin to act accordingly. In other words, if you throw me out, for whatever reason, I may come back but the memory of you throwing me out will remain for quite possibly, the rest of my days – and not only that. The memory may resurface to the front of my consciousness at any time and make me start feeling or acting some type of way toward you because of that fact.

Contingency Based Goodness

A common relationship way of life is the 'don't make me stop doing what I'm doing, if you're not going to stop doing what you are doing' thing. What this commonly means is that the individuals involved in the relationship are whores and their whore stoppage is contingent upon the whore stoppage of the individual they are involved in the relationship with or about to become involved in a relationship with. Now don't take offense if this applies to any of you reading. People say because they hate labels, that they are just living life or what has been commonly relayed to me, 'I'm doing me.' Okay, here's the thing: if you are sleeping around, even if it is with the intent to find Mr. or Miss Right, you are a whore because that's what whores do. Good girls don't sleep around and neither do good guys. Now please understand, I'm not judging by any means, for heaven's sake, I used to do it. (A lot) But I am just calling a spade a spade. Now the thought process of these people AKA whores usually resembles 'when I get into a relationship I will be 'good.' In other words 'I will be faithful. I will go cold turkey in regard to my previous activities of sleeping with any and everybody I want to.' Now the thing about this cold turkey promise or intention is that as honorable as it may seem at the time, few people in this world are actually capable of accomplishing it. And one of the biggest beliefs about this belief is the one, which states that if one individual in the relationship can go cold turkey in regard to sleeping with other random individuals, then the other individual in the relationship should be able to as well. In addition to that fact, so many people are basing their decision to be 'good' on how 'good' the other partner is to them. This is why so many relationships fail. People cannot be 'good' with stipulations. Either you are a good individual or you are not. People cannot say 'as long as you don't cheat on me, I won't cheat on you' and the reason why is because that type of thinking basically leaves a person on the verge of committing an indiscretion right up until the other commits an indiscretion of his or her own. You see these people are giving the significant others all of the power in the relationship. They are doing so by responding to what they do and using that response as guidelines for how their own life should go. They are not saying 'I should be good because it's the right thing to do.' They are saying 'I'm only going to be good if you are.' My question is this: how can you make anyone else in this world responsible for your level of good or bad? If you want to be a whore, as what the above behavior clearly dictates, then claim it! Say it loud, say it proud, 'I'm a whore! And I don't need anyone else to take accountability for me or my actions.' But you see the problem is that people know the difference between right and wrong. They know that sleeping around is frowned on, whether you are in a relationship or not. But see they just want to have somebody else to place the blame on when things go wrong. They want to be able to say 'I was faithful to you and you fucked up! You brought me to this point! You made me cheat!' Now granted, if an individual in a relationship cheats and gets caught by the significant other, yes, you can obviously say that he or she fucked up. But here's the thing: nobody can make you pull your dick out and stick it into another woman. And on the opposite end of the spectrum nobody can make you allow a dick to be stuffed into you either, except yourself. These decisions are made on your own. Lack of morals, lack of proper home training and lack of control are definitely contributing factors but the bottom line is that the decision is yours and yours alone. As stated before people cannot or do not want to accept responsibility for their actions so they figure 'I'll just blame the relationship, or the other party.' And this is why as soon as one individual in a relationship cheats, the most thought of option for either relationship correction or happiness within themselves, is to cheat on that no good bastard or bitch as revenge. A good rule of thumb for how you should act in relationships is this: if you cannot do what you did before the relationship, after the relationship commences, then you should not be doing it at all. In other words, if you cannot sleep with two, three or seven guys after you become committed, then you should not do it before you begin to think about being committed. One reason is because people will see you and not only that, they will remember and will eventually bring that up to either you or the one you are planning a future with. Another reason is because it will be that much harder to rid yourself of the two, three or seven person mindset once you become involved. As stated above, everybody can have good intentions on going cold turkey when it comes to forgetting their whorish past but not everybody is capable – especially when things get difficult. What people have to start realizing is that when in a relationship, their actions are no longer for them. They have to live for another individual. When you are alone, you can burp as loud as you want but when you get involved, the significant other may expect you to stop. When you are alone you can curse and be as abrasive as you desire but when you become involved, the man you are with may say that's not ladylike. This rule of thumb further dictates that you should think first for the actual or potential significant other and how your actions may or will affect them before you do those actions, especially infidelity.

This point cannot be stated enough: <u>relationships contain deception.</u> The amount will be great or it will be miniscule but relationships contain some form of deceit. Either there is deception perpetrated against the parties involved in the relationship or there is deception perpetrated against society by those in the relationship. When it comes to the deception perpetrated by those in relationships toward each other, the standard operating procedure is as follows: It is not so much I am in this relationship because I love this man or woman, as much as it is I need this man or woman. Necessity, in case any of you are unaware, will always win out over love. The problem with this is that the idea behind necessity is need. I need you. The problem with that is that most people interpret need as use. So on the one hand you have people not wanting to give all of themselves because they think that the others are doing nothing but using them. On the other hand, you have people who are just using the others, doing so under the guise of love. So when people go into a relationship half heartedly, it can many times be understood. Some of these people are doing little more than protecting their hearts. Now it is often suggested that when involving one's self in a new relationship, an individual should protect his or her heart at all times but the thing that almost everybody in a new relationship wants is for the other to give his or her heart completely to them. See the problem? If you give all of your heart to somebody you don't know, you open yourself up to being vulnerable. If you don't completely open up or give yourself to the one you are in a relationship with, he or she will more than likely believe that you are being deceptive by hiding something. So what's a person to do? You see, this is why relationships are considered games. You have to divulge only so much to the person you decide to give your life to. Knowledge of one's life is many times given on a need to know basis. In other words, if I think you need to know this about me, I will let you know. Not a fair exchange if you ask me. But here's the thing about that: many times, the way an individual acts is directly due to events in an individual's past. And if a person does not know or understand the past of the individual he or she is in a relationship with, it will be exceptionally difficult to understand the present or the future. You see this goes back to complete trust and getting to know. When you get to know <u>all you can</u> about somebody and you <u>trust them completely</u> then you can divulge everything about yourself. The only problem with this: you will never know anybody completely. The most you can ever hope to know about somebody is a good portion. If people knew everything about the significant other, then they would never have to worry about the significant other one day flipping out and trying to kill them. If they knew everything about the significant other, then they would never have to worry about making the other mad because they would already know what not to do. But you see, getting to know an individual is a <u>lifelong process.</u> Nobody in any relationship can say that he or she knows everything about the husband or wife. The more you know however, the better chance you will have at the relationship lasting more than just a few months or years. Parents can have a child for twenty years and still not know everything about that child, although many of them disillusion themselves into thinking that they do. So how can you reasonably expect that after a certain amount of time, you will know everything about the person you are sleeping with? When people need you, they will do whatever it takes to get and keep you. The problem with this is that this philosophy is exactly the same as love. If I love you, then I will do whatever it takes to keep you. See the similarity? Now people are quick to say that when it comes to deception, they can easily weed out that deception because they can feel true love. They can feel it in their hearts. But see, this is why deception is so prevalent and powerful. It is the same feeling an individual gets when he or she is deep in the stronghold of love. When you think with your head while in a relationship, people will get confused by your actions. Often they will call you stubborn and they will think that you are being unnecessarily difficult because your actions are based on logic as opposed to emotion. People expect that when you are in love, you will do what everybody else who is in love, has done or will do as well. People expect that you will get married because you are in love. Then they will expect you to have kids because you are in love. Then they will continue to expect you to go through a certain protocol because this is what people in love do. But if you say you are in love and you don't get married, then it becomes 'he's playing you for a fool' or 'she doesn't love you.' Then it becomes if you're married for a few years and you don't have kids, something is wrong with one or both of you or there is turmoil in the relationship. People don't stop to think that maybe earning and saving enough money before you make a life altering decision like having kids is the smart thing to do. They think that because you don't follow a certain society imposed protocol, then your life is not as happy as it could or should be.

Chapter

2

Everybody Lies In A Relationship

Everybody lies in a relationship. If this is not the truest and at the same time most controversial comment in history, then I don't know what is. Lies are what is commonly referred to as deception. And deception, just in case any of you are unaware, is thought to be one of man's greatest weapons. Deception is used so much in relationships that many would not be able to exist in a relationship if it were not there. The problem with this statement is that many who are deceived, have no idea that they are. People will always say that their relationship is full of truth and honesty and whatever else but this is the power that deception has. It is the fact that people do not know if and when they are deceived, which allows deception to continue. Now one of the biggest lies, which will occur in relationships is the basic one of what we want in the relationship or what we want for the relationship. Guys will say that they do not want just sex. Women will say that they do. But once sex is had, everything gets flipped. Guys will say that yes you were right, all I wanted was the sex and the females will say they don't want to have sex all the time. This is because the initial deception was only enough to begin the relationship, not sustain it.

Now one of the most prevalent occurrences or lies, depending upon your perspective, is how people will start out fucking and then decide later that they fell for the individual they were fucking. This is commonly known as catching feelings. Now for those who may not know, feelings are the most feared by product of any relationship. And the reason why is because feelings never die. They just fluctuate in intensity. And also for those who may not know, in regard to the above scenario, the feelings were always there, it just took a minute for the individuals to catch up and realize. Now the reason this is so bad is because, like you really need to be told this, the natural order of things is being done in reverse. You are supposed to fall in love and then have sex. People are using their twisted logic to say things like 'I was fucking her for the longest and you know everything was fine but then she caught feelings and now she don't wanna let me go' or this dude and I were fuck buddies then all of a sudden he starts telling me that 'I'm his and I can't talk to nobody else and so on and so forth.' You see this is why relationships continue to fail. Sex, which is supposed to be one of the most important parts of a relationship, is being had all willy nilly, as if the participants are nothing but two out of control teenagers. So my question is did these people fall in love with the sex or did they fall in love because of the sex? Think about the possible ramifications of this type of relationship: sex is being had just because the two participants are sexually compatible. One pops up pregnant. Now a relationship is forced because a child is involved. And nine times out of ten, the couple did not want their relationship to go any further than sex. So what happens now is a man, who probably had no other interest in a particular woman than bending her over a table or two, has to pretend to like said woman or vice versa just because the woman has a child. If the only connection the two of these individuals have is the child, they are going to be beyond miserable trying to deal with each other on a relationship basis. And the reason why is because this couple does not know anything about each other besides being sex buddies. They do not know the likes, dislikes, quirks or idiosyncrasies of the other individual. So what this boils down to is basically two strangers trying to raise a child and at the same time build a relationship, instead of two strangers getting to know one another, first, building a relationship and then preparing for the possibility of a child. Now I know that there will be at least one person saying something to the effect of 'you're never really ready for a child.' And that is a true statement. Children do test the hell out of your patience and emotional stability, as well as idea of preparedness, but here's the thing: when you have an idea that a child is a potential possibility or a planned event, it makes the transition from single person to parent a whole helluva lot easier.

When it comes to lying in relationships, what people have to do is find out is why the significant other chose to lie in the first place. Once the reasons behind the lies and deception are disclosed, often the reasons for the lies can be understood. Now I do not mean to say that if there is a good enough reason, then the lie should be accepted. I am just saying that certain situations will make a person act outside of his or her character. Now let's examine the two main reasons most people have for telling a lie. They are to escape consequences and to protect feelings. In a relationship, these two reasons are tweaked ever so slightly to include escaping consequences from the significant other and to protect the feelings of the significant other. There are other situations in which people feel they have to lie to the significant other and one of those highly popular reasons is the one of finances. With poverty and low income jobs being as much of an issue as they are, many people who make more than their counterparts or lovers, will never completely divulge the truth in relationships regarding what and how much they earn. Many times these people will straight up lie because people will base the amount of like they have for another solely on the amount of money he or she makes and receives from the other. And this is because society has made it almost a crime to be involved with somebody on a different financial level, if this individual is not giving all of his or her money to the other who may not be on the same financial level as the first. You see, the way the thought process of society is, will make it seem like if one makes $100k per year and the man or woman he or she is involved with, makes $21k per year, the one making $100k must always be the one to take the other on vacations, pay bills, pay for the other's upkeep, basically keep the other out of financial ruin. Now quite often this is a gender issue because no matter who makes the most, the highly popularized belief is that the man should always be taking care of the woman. This will create a problem because sooner or later someone in their infinite wisdom will impart the idea into the mind of the individual making the most that a relationship is 50/50 and all that and by you being the one to provide all of the financial disbursement, you are allowing yourself to be taken advantage of. In addition to that, there is the worry that due to the imperfection of the human spirit, there is always the possibility that the significant other may set up the one who makes more or a lot more money in the relationship to be robbed or worse. There are also going to be many people who read this who will say that a man or woman in a relationship setting up the one he or she is involved in a relationship with to be a victim of a crime is an impossibility but people will do anything in this world and if sex, which I believe to be one of the deepest and most important parts of a relationship, can be had after knowing somebody for all of two days, how hard is it to believe that the above criminal activity is not feasible?

What should be known when it comes to lying in a relationship, is that a person is only going to be as honest as much as he or she feels comfortable. If an individual knows that there will be certain ramifications for certain types of honesty, then that person will do or say whatever to avoid those certain ramifications. If a man knows that there is going to be an argument after he tells his woman that he has been at the club, when he knows that she does not like him going to the club, do you think he's going to be honest and tell her that he was at the club? Of course not. If that same man has spent all of his money, which was supposed to be used for bills, again, do you think he will tell? Again of course not. You see lying is a response but it is also a defense. In relationships, what too many people do is focus on the fact that a lie was told instead of the reason why it was told. Now there will always be those who will say that there can never be a justifiable reason to tell a lie. Now I have tried to understand as these people do but my level of thinking always turns me back around to there is always a reason to lie. Sometimes that reason is to protect a loved one or family member. Now sure people can always tell the truth and potentially cause severe harm or detriment to a significant other or family member but who in his or her right mind want to do that?

If the average   individual is in trouble, and the only way he or she can get out of trouble is to tweak the truth ever so slightly, I am sure that most of you would be in agreement when I say that that particular individual more than likely would. If it were a family member, damn near everybody in this world would lie to ensure that family member's safety. So this thing of lying can be understood. It is just not universally accepted. There are certain situations where a lie is appropriate (as above) and there are certain situations where lies are only good at causing more detriment to the individual telling. And the biggest or most common situation of a lie causing detriment, is the one of an individual being caught lying about the opposite sex. Here's the thing: when it comes to a person in a relationship lying about the opposite sex, the belief will be that the only reason is because there is something derogatory going on. The belief will be that either the significant other is screwing the one being lied about, wants to screw the one being lied about or has already screwed the one being lied about. There is no lying about the opposite sex without there being some element of sexual activity or gratification. It just doesn't happen. Now there are instances where the one being lied about is an actual, platonic friend and the significant other does not like the friend and wants the other to stay away because there is a fear that something in his or her mind may be going on. In situations such as this, lying can be understood. The reason is because in too many relationships today, people want to control the activities of the significant other. They want to many times control the significant other from where he or she goes, to whom he or she goes to see. And if a person deals with somebody like this, they damned sure will not tell the jealous or crazy significant other that they are doing so. You see many times in relationships, it becomes a choice between lifelong friends and the significant other. Many people feel that they don't want to give up their contacts and associates from many years back, so they try to have their cake and eat it to, so to speak. They will keep friends who the significant other may not like, without the significant other's knowledge. And sometimes, many times in fact, these friends include the ex of the significant other.

Lies are meant to be confusing. And one of the biggest types of confusion is the unwritten law that states people cannot always be held accountable for lying to the significant other if they do not know what they are doing is telling a lie. Now many people will surely wonder how can anyone not know the difference between a lie and the truth. And that is a valid question. The thing, which I have noticed, is that what people do not intend to be a lie many times comes across as one. This is what is known as an unintentional lie. Now an example of an unintentional lie is something that almost all of us do. It is 'honey, I just left the job' when in actuality, you have been on the train or bus for half an hour. You see while one individual's interpretation of just left is two, three or even five minutes ago, another's interpretation of a lie could be you said you just left but that was 30 minutes ago. People let these types of misinterpretations happen and cause arguments all the time. This is an example of my way of thinking should be your way of thinking – and since we know it will never be, unnecessary arguments and misinterpretations will continue to destroy relationships. Now it is not the fact that people lie so much in relationships, as it is the fact of what people lie about which cause detriment. As stated above, when people lie about the opposite sex, there will be instant thoughts of raucous behavior and debauchery. When people lie about children, for instance, before a relationship was initiated, or even children who came about after a relationship was underway, there will be thoughts of them being ashamed of having children, them ashamed of not taking care of their children or them not knowing who the actual parent is. In any case, deception of this type will show that the one perpetrating the deception is not really relationship material. When people continue to lie or lie with seemingly no reason for doing so, the other will believe that the one telling the lies are not capable of telling the truth.

Many times in relationships, there will be those confusing lying episodes that are basically indistinguishable from the truth. These episodes will make so much of the truth sound like a lie and so much of a lie sound like the truth that many in relationships will believe a lie over the truth. An example of this is 'baby I was cheating on you with the girl you saw me in the picture with.' Another example of this is 'I fell asleep due to drinking a lot and some girl went in my pocket and took out my phone, then laid down next to me and snapped a picture of me and her together – but I don't know who she is.' Now the thing about these two scenarios is that one is the truth and one is the lie. The disturbing thing about these two scenarios is that the one, which sounds like the lie, the second one, is the truth – and the first one, which is more easily believable, is the lie. When a person is under the influence, how easy is it to get this person in hot water with his significant other, especially when his significant other is one who has issues with trust to begin with? I know because the above situation happened to me. Some young girl thought it would be funny if she used my phone to take a picture of me and her sleeping. When I told my girl, who went through my phone for no conceivable good reason, the absolute truth, which was I have no idea who this girl was, do you think she believed me? Hell fucking no! She had already made it up in her mind and nothing short of an act of God would allow her to change her thinking. This is why if you do not have trust in the beginning of your relationship, there is a strong possibility that you never will.

I truly believe that out of all of the unfortunate circumstances which can occur in a relationship, one of the most damaging is not an actual occurrence but a belief. This belief is that somewhere in a galaxy far, far away, people are capable of complete honesty in a relationship. Okay maybe that came out a little premature. People are completely capable of complete honesty. They just cannot always handle it. Anybody can say 'I don't like you, I just want to fuck you.' But the question, which needs to be asked, is how successful will that individual be in his pursuits? People have to use tact and sensitivity when they are perpetrating deception or else the harshness, which few are equipped to handle, will scare the significant other or potential significant other off. Now in regard to the above, it is probably the safest bet in the world that nobody will accept that – but you see when a person has the opportunity to have sex with probably the best looking person he or she has ever seen and the only thing stopping the act from occurring is a few untrue words, do you really think everybody will have the moral fortitude or consciousness of mind to do what's right? Or will they lie to accomplish their goal, which is fuck the shit out of this mf and deal with the ramifications later? You see, one of the biggest lies, which is ironically perpetrated by those who expect complete honesty is the one of 'no matter how it hurts, please tell me the truth. I can handle it.' This is ironic simply because one of the main rules for happiness or longevity in relationships is to hurt the significant other as little as possible but yet the relaying of complete honesty has long been known to hurt. Do you see the hypocrisy here? If I tell the truth, I hurt you, but to keep you happy in a relationship, I am not supposed to hurt you. But if I tell you a lie, and you find out about it, then that will hurt you and make you unhappy. So what this boils down to is I have to lie but not let you find out that I'm telling a lie or lie, but make it sound so well that you will have no choice but to believe that it is truth because the truth, which sounds so much like a lie these days, will hurt you and since I am not supposed to do that, what other option do I have? Now to understand why lying and deceptive practices are so prevalent in relationships, we should take a peek into the motivating factors behind why lying is perpetrated in the first place. In addition to the above stated reasons of protecting feelings and escaping consequences, there is one other category, which prompts people to lie and that is the one of benefits – and no, not just the sexual kind. When a person lies, many times the individual who is being lied to already expects to hear a certain type of response – and if the one who is lying answers in the manner that the other is expecting, he or she will be able to recoup all of those benefits, whether they be financial, or a place in the other's heart. You see, all some people need another to do is say the right things and that person will be the epitome of the other's love and affection – even though the other may many times say always tell me the truth.

When it comes to relationships, some people in this world lie simply because they know that divulging the truth about a particular person or situation will put their lives in a certain amount of jeopardy. True, there are some individuals who will say that they live the kind of lives where there is no room for lying and no situation will ever cause them to lie but my question is what about what happens when someone cheats? And not only that, what about the ramifications of that infidelity? Here's the thing: people are going to lie when they cheat. That's a verified fact. I don't think any cheater in this world is going to go say 'honey, I'm about to go and fuck somebody, okay?' If they did, they would not be called cheaters, they would be called swingers – and their partner would be accompanying them. But let's say that this particular cheater feels remorse about his or her actions and tries to come clean about the affair. If the cheater tells the truth about the affair, which is many times desired and often respected, nine times out of ten, he or she will remain silent about a child or children which were made as a result of the affair. And the reason why there will be this silence or withholding of facts about the outside of the relationship offspring, is because there is <u>no</u> acceptance when it comes to taking care of somebody else's child or allowing a significant other to do so while in a relationship with that significant other. It's just not done. Wait, it is done but it is not respected. Ask yourself, do you really think any wife in this world is going to say 'yeah honey you cheated on me and you had a child with some other bitch, but as long as you take care of your responsibilities, I'm okay with it.' Hell fucking no. This woman is more than likely going to kill him or try her best to make sure that some kind of retribution is dispersed. And this is not one of those gender dependent occurrences here either. A man will more than likely have the same type of adverse feeling and negative outlook toward the woman who has cheated. The only thing I have seen different is the type of responses. Whereas women who cheat, whether they have a child through the infidelity or not, they will not become the 'whore of Babylon' type of individual. Men for some reason or other will do it more and will use the fact that the other has cheated as justification for their inability to control themselves. If women have a child outside of the relationship, they will either try for a relationship with the parent of that child, if the original relationship ends due to the affair. They will not sleep around with everybody they can get their hands on unless it is due to some underlying mental disorder. At least from what I have seen. Now while on the topic of this, there are many women who will lie and tell a man that he is the father of a child when he is not. This falls under the category of benefits. The main benefit is the one of the woman gets a child and somebody to take care of the child and the only thing she has to do is keep up the façade of letting the man believe what any man in a relationship would believe anyway. I mean why else would a man have doubt about a child being his from the woman he has given his heart to unless the woman had been deceptive all along? Now sometimes this scenario is not always the fault of the woman. Wait it is but it is not always intentional. Some women practice what I like to call free love. In other words, they are what are commonly referred to as sluts. They will sleep with a lot of men and in all honesty believe that the one person they lay claim to is actually the father. This could be an honest mistake. It says nothing for her credibility as far as being a person of high moral character but mistakes do happen. Then what we have is a situation of do I believe her? Was she lying all along or did she make an honest mistake? This extends to if I get involved with her after the fact, will I ever be able to believe her when it comes to her not being a slut or anything else for that matter? You see the reason or reasons women lie about kids belonging to someone other than the actual father is aside from the benefit of having someone there to take care of the child, they do not want the actual father in the life of the child. People have sex for money. They have sex because they are forced to. They have sex because they want to trick the one they are having sex with into believing that they are in love as opposed to being used for whatever it is they may need at the time. This is also known as being trifling as shit. Again this is not always intentional. People often have sex with no idea of the ramifications. Then when ramifications occur, people respond in the most reactive manner imaginable. All of these reasons and more are why some women will give the title of daddy to someone else. There is also the fact that some of the men these women decide to sleep with are violent as shit and are in no way marriage material or parenting material. Women will lie and say 'it's your baby' to somebody who is marriage material or parenting material so that they can have a comfortable upbringing for their child. This is a somewhat noble thought but what people need to remember is that the practice of lying contains no nobility. This is what people have to understand. This is what goes back to the basic lesson of don't sleep with anybody you do not want to marry.

Here's a question for those of you who believe that there is no place in a relationship for a lie: if the first time you and a significant other have sex and it is not stellar, do you tell this individual well it wasn't the best I've had or do you use tact and say it was good, I loved it! Next time let's try this to make it even better? Only cold hearted and callous individuals will say 'the sex was bad, you can't fuck' and things of that nature. You see people who want to stay in a relationship will do the one thing that people who do not want to be in a relationship don't and that is try to keep the relationship afloat by any means necessary. For those of you who do not know, this includes lying. Now what many people who lie to the significant other will many times say is I do not lie or accept lying in my relationship. I just help my relationship by not divulging the complete truth (as in the example above) but what these people do not realize is that this is deception by omission. AKA being deceptive by not telling the significant other what it is he or she needs to hear. AKA not telling the truth. But we all know what this is: this is softening the blow so that the response from the significant other is one that can be easily handled. I mean honestly who wants to say something to the effect of 'sorry honey your dick is no good' and then have the significant other respond angrily with something to the effect of 'maybe it's your pussy that ain't no good!' And so on and so on. This is what one could call defensive relationshipping. It is just like defensive driving where an individual has to prepare for the actions of another based on the actions of the first, even before the first makes a move. With the relationshipping thing, you have to think 'I know he or she will more than likely respond in this manner, if I come at them in this manner, so I have to make them respond the way I want them to even before I say anything.' Yes, this is a high degree of manipulation but many times that high degree of manipulation is exactly what relationships are. People will lie about how good the sex is in a relationship in order to keep a relationship. This is what one could call relationship deception protocol. Again, relationships are about expectations and deception. People expect to have sex in a relationship. They expect that whatever sex is had in the relationship will always be good. In fact great. Nobody expects that the sex act will be anything less than stellar – least of all the participants in the relationship. But here's where the deception comes in: if everything else in the relationship is going fine, meaning the bills are all paid, there is an ample amount of money in savings, as well as in the pockets of both parties in the relationship, there is a decent amount of communication between the two and the kids are well taken care of, do any of you in your right minds think that either significant other is going to even risk jeopardizing the lifestyle to which they are both accustomed by complaining about the sex? Of course not. But see, here's the crazy thing: many times the significant other who is unsatisfied, will more than likely seek sexual fulfillment elsewhere. Yes, the significant other will jeopardize his or her relationship by indulging in an affair but he or she will never tell the significant other he or she is unhappy with the sex. It is something about that fragile ego thing. Now don't misunderstand me, because there are several cold hearted bastards in this world who will grasp the first and every opportunity to say 'you got a baby dick' or calling the significant other 'canyon pussy' because the sex is not up to par but from my experience, those that do, really do not care much about the longevity of the relationship.

Chapter

3

Love Is A Four Letter Word And So Is Shit

Many people are raised with the belief that the basis for all relationships is love. They are raised to believe that whatever love they have when a relationship is initiated, will be shared by whomever it is they decide to deal with. These people are even raised to believe that relationships are guaranteed to last just because they have been initiated. Do you feel as sorry for these misguided souls as I do? You should. You see, to many people in this world, a relationship is little more than a twelve letter word. To these people, a relationship carries along with it nothing more than the fact that it involves another person. These types of people are prevalent in the relationship world because the people who know better, who want the complete and total opposite of what these other people seem to want, continue to get into relationships with them. And therein lies the problem. You see, no matter what people may try and have you believe, relationships are all about perception. They are about what I want and what I think you want.

It does not matter what the other party in the relationship actually wants – only about what the prevailing decision maker wants for both parties. You see this is why relationships are phony. This is why relationships are full of shit. This is why relationships are about control. Here's an example: for the longest of time, many girls have been reared to fit into the good girl classification. What this means is that once they become adults, they are expected to be married first and foremost, adequately take care of their families second, and never, ever leave those families. On the other end of the spectrum, many guys have been reared to fit into the bad boy classification. What this means is that along with guys being taught to do everything that a 'good' person who follows the rules, sits up straight and respects women, does not do, bad guys are taught to fuck as many girls as they can and if one pops up pregnant, then that one becomes either the wife or the child support recipient. The two genders have different criteria regarding what will make the other marriage material and it is not so much separated by gender, as it is by the individual. Every man has a different criteria list for what he deems important in his ideal woman and every woman has her own as well. The only problem in relationships is that neither party will tell the other what they want, need and expect from the other, so that the other can act the part. They just expect the other to know and totally flip out or cheat when the other doesn't. You see this is why you have women crying their eyes out and contemplating suicide when the guy they gave their heart and vagina to does not want to marry them. You see, this is why you have guys doing the hundred yard dash in the opposite direction when a woman relays to them that they want to get married after a certain amount of time together. You see what people in relationships do is get together under the jb statute. What is jb you ask? Just because. They get together just because the other is attractive. They get together just because the other has money. They get together just because the other is someone that a bff or family member has suggested will be a good fit or good catch for a relationship. These people more than likely have no idea what it takes to keep the relationship going past the sexual aspect of the relationship. And the unfortunate thing about that is they don't care. This is why people have to trick the one they are interested in, into a long term relationship, sexual or otherwise. It is because deception is what many relationships are based on but it is deception under the guise of love. Guys have to be deceptive to get into women's pants. Women have to be deceptive to get into guys hearts. Kinda messed up ain't it? But this is how the relationship game is played. There is no more complete love and honesty. It has been replaced with deception and treachery. In addition to getting together because of the jb statute, many of these people who are living under the impression that there relationship is going to eventually turn out the way they want it to, will get married under what is called the might as well statute. This is the label or reasoning given to people who get married for no feasible reason. They say things like you've been together for so long, you might as well get married. Or you already have kids, so you might as well get married. Or,

'you love him?'

'yes'

'well then you might as well get married.'

It is about the biggest shame imaginable that people are not fully able to read these lines and see that this reasoning for involving ones self in a lifelong commitment is bullshit. But yet people use might as well and the jb statue as relationship initiation and continuation all the time. And then they wanna wonder why their relationships go straight to shit. You see what people have to get into their thick, fucking skulls is that love is not the same thing for everybody. My interpretation of love is not your interpretation of love. It is the same thing with happiness. I could be happy smacking you upside the head everyday, but I'm will to bet that you as the receiver of the smacks, would be somewhat discontent. You see until people realize that love is only as strong as it's interpretation, and marriage is only as strong as the feelings and interpretation each person in the marriage have for it, they will never mean anything more than words and a piece of paper. People say the words I love you but then they go out and cheat. What? Is I love you supposed to stop them from cheating? Newsflash! It doesn't and it won't. People get married all the time and are expected to act in the same manner as how other married people act or in the same manner as the significant other expects them to act but nine times out of ten, you do not know this person. What you know is your hopes and dreams and expectancy of how this person will act for the rest of his or her life. This is the problem. Nine times out of ten, the people getting married under the guise of love have little to no concept of what that word entails one; for you and two; for the relationship. When you have your interpretation of love and you try to impose it upon the significant other or upon somebody you hope will be the significant other, you are setting yourself up for heartbreak. The unfortunate part about this scenario is that when you tell somebody what you want and expect in a relationship, quite often you are doing the same thing. You see people will many times use deception and by this, they will listen to want you want and expect in a relationship, and then they will act the part. In other words, they will agree and basically tell you what you want to hear or do what you want them to do. You know the ole slight variation on what it is you have already told them. To extract truth from somebody when it comes to what they want from an individual in a relationship or what they want regarding taking care of a child and family, or even what it is they want regarding love, ask them first! Ask them what is their interpretation of love. Ask them what do they want from a significant other, and don't just accept generic, textbook things like, I want somebody who loves me for me and somebody who will put me first and yada, yada. Ask them what they will do in the relationship and challenge them to do it before you get into the relationship. This is called getting to know. Too many people accept the first thing the other says, which sounds even remotely like something that they want for themselves in the relationship and run with it. A person says 'I love you and I will always love you' or 'when I love somebody I love hard' and the next thing you know a relationship is born. This is bullshit and do you know why? It's because speaking the word love is meaningless. You first have to know what it is you want from love. You have to know what your definition of love is. Then you have to meet somebody who has the same definition or pretty damned close to yours before you even think about dropping your drawers. People have to realize that deception is not just a one time thing. Often it can last throughout the entirety of the relationship. What causes people's relationships to many times fail is that aside from getting involved with people they don't know and expecting to get to grow to know this individual, they get involved based on what they want and what they think the other person in the relationship wants. This is not love. This is deception. You see the truly sad thing about relationships is the fact that people mistakenly love the actions of an individual more so that the individual they are involved with. Now granted, actions in a relationship are important. But they are nothing when compared to actually loving the person for who he or she is. This world is so screwed up that if someone buys a five thousand dollar ring for another, then almost as if by magic, the other will consider himself or herself in love with that individual. If one person buys the other a car or some expensive item that he or she would never have been able to acquire themselves, again, enter the belief that this individual is in love. It is even the same thing with sex. When there is good, rather great sex, (sex is always good) many who cannot differentiate between great sex and love will feel that the individual who provided the great sex loves them and that's why they provided the great sex. But here's the thing: people love the action, instead of the person and this is why if your relationship has not failed, it will surely do so soon. Relationships, whether people want to admit it or not, are about deception. They are about making the other believe that he or she is the best person in the world for the one he or she is involved in the relationship with. For many people, love is the same thing. It is a word. It is a word, which has as many different meanings as there are people to interpret those meanings. The problem with this is that no two people have the exact same interpretation of the word love and of the word relationship. The bigger problem is trying to get two people together who have as close to the same interpretation of both of these two words as possible and make the relationship work. Do you now see why deception is a much more desired option? It is just easier to fake a relationship than to go through all of the trouble of making the relationship work.

You see, what too many people do is get into relationships like they get into cars. And they stay in both as long as they are going well. As soon as a problem arises, then they want to either learn about the relationship, or the car, or take them both to get fixed. Here's the thing: if people learn all about a car, from how to change a tire, to how to change the oil and more, then they would not have to spend money going to outsiders for help. If people did the same thing in relationships, again, they would not have to go to outsiders for help. But you see people do not think this far. They never think this far. All most individuals want to do is enjoy the perks of ownership. They seem to want to be able to say 'I have a car' or 'I have a relationship' and nothing else. Then they want to wonder why their relationships and vehicles always happen to fail.

The bottom line here is that love by itself, will never make a relationship. Love by itself will break a relationship however. And it will do this because without the continued effort necessary to keep the relationship alive, love is little more than a very strong feeling of attraction. The expectation that most have when it comes to relationships is what will kill those relationships. There are those who get involved in relationships and expect that the significant other will come home on Thursday or whatever day payday is and give the other half of the received pay. The other may be totally unaware of this expectation. But here's the thing: many in this world are groomed to believe that that is the definition of taking care of the other. People have to lay down the rules in a relationship because a relationship is not two people happily meeting one another and staying happy for the rest of their days. A relationship is 'I need you to tell me what it is I'm walking into, so that years down the line, I don't wake up one day and want to slap the shit out of you because you come at me with some crazy bullshit like what was explained above.' The problem is that people are far too often under the impression that you can only tell the other so much truth at one time. They figure that the longer they are together, the more love there is in the relationship, hence the more opportunity they will have to spring unmentioned stuff on the significant other and he or she will have but no choice to accept and comply. Knowledge of what an individual desires for his or her life is paramount. It is what's needed before an individual can even think about going to look for a significant other. That way an individual can be confident in asking the man or woman of their dreams for help in achieving it. The problem, which causes many to say I always keep picking the wrong man or woman, is that some of us have no fucking idea what it is we want for the long term. Women do not relay to the men they get involved with that they will eventually want the man to cook dinner every once in a while when they themselves do not feel like cooking and not just bring home Chinese food and think that that will suffice. Men don't really say to the women they get involved with 'I want you to be like my mother, you know with the no cursing policy and the keeping a clean house and cooking all the time and basically multitasking to superhuman levels.' People expect that – and they expect it forever. We too often only know immediate gratification, things which are going to make us happy now. We have no idea what is to be included in a five or ten year plan because we almost never think about being in a relationship that long. The only thing people unfortunately think about regarding a relationship is that the relationship is going to last forever, without any work on the part of the people involved – until of course, it doesn't.

Chapter

4

Anger Issues

Anger is a loss of control. A loss of control is what I believe everybody in this world has experienced at one time or another. With that being said, a loss of control is not a part of any healthy relationship. One can become upset, perturbed, even mad at the significant other but once the feelings of what should be in the relationship and how they should be handled travel all the way to anger, it can be seen as passing the point of no return. Having control is the ability to restrict hurtful comments. It is being able to communicate rationally about things that are upsetting to one or both parties in the relationship. It is never letting your feelings get the best of you. When people lose control however, many have been known to not just verbally abuse the significant other, but curse him or her the fuck out at the drop of a hat. They have been known to throw things and a few have even been known to become physically aggressive. Now the problem with this whole anger thing is that nobody can make anybody become that angry to the point where they react in a manner such as above. They allow themselves to become angry to that point. That is what causes them to react in the manners described above. Some people feel that the best way to handle a situation when the significant other does something stupid or something that can only be interpreted as being intentionally done to cause harm or unhappiness, is to do the exact thing they did back to them. For instance, they hit you, hit them back. They cheat on you, cheat on them. They look at you with what you interpret as threatening or even disdain, then you look at them the same way. The problem with this is that nine times out of ten, your interpretation of their actions are completely wrong and by you basing your reactions on your mistaken interpretations of their actions, you are often causing more detriment than what is necessary. And a prime example of this is the he looked at me mean, so I have to look back at him just as mean. But sometimes people just have an expression, which can be interpreted as mean and by you responding to your thought, the other will think that you are initiating violence and then he will respond to your action. This brings up the simple thought of what is so hard about giving a smile? It doesn't make you less of a man to do this. The problem with this is that people feel if they are nice, then others will think that they are not tough. And for some people not being tough or not being seen as tough, is about the biggest sin that can be committed. Now anger comes from many places. It can come from dealing with the present relationship. It can come from childhood issues, which were never resolved. It can even come from issues with the opposite sex, which occurred way before the present relationship came to fruition. But here's the thing: no matter where the anger comes from, it is within you and you have to be the one to be able to control it. I remember listening to one of those talk show therapists one time and he said one of the most profound things I had heard in quite a while. He said that if you were to squeeze an orange, no matter how hard you squeezed, no matter how much pressure was applied, the only thing that would come out was orange juice. And this was because the orange juice was the only thing that was inside. You would never get grape juice or any other kind of juice simply because it was never in there to begin with. If people could emulate this, meaning if there was no anger inside of a person, then it would never be able to come out. But see, here's the thing: people do not realize how the anger issues they do have will affect anybody until they come out and make themselves known. People don't realize how the anger issues they may have will affect the opposite sex in the relationship until the opposite sex is affected. The problem with this is that many who have these unresolved anger issues don't really think that their issues with anger are anything above or different than what the average individual goes through when he or she gets mad. People will say everybody gets mad once in a while and since I didn't kill anybody or hurt anybody, then I guess my anger was within acceptable levels. And this is because people are rarely taught any textbook spectrum levels of what acceptable behavior is when it comes to being upset and angry. People figure, 'okay I made her mad and she cursed at me, it's okay, I deserved it.' Or they will say 'he choked me because I was disrespectful to him.' And these are not made up examples either. These are what people have relayed to me about their relationships. Now in case any of you reading this may be confused about how acceptable any of the above actions are, let me tell you; they are wrong. They are wrong. They are wrong. You do not curse and use profanity at the person you love when he or she makes you mad. When you do, you are teaching the lesson that everything you do up to the boiling point is okay. You are teaching the lesson that instead of me putting a stop to behavior, which will surely escalate, I will wait until I cannot take it anymore and then respond with what I think is me getting upset but everybody else interpreting it as a loss of control. Instead of one trying to deescalate the situation before it even has a chance to get to the point of me choking the life out of the other, I will only respond with violence. Now this is not always the fault of those in relationships. And this is because people are almost never taught how to deescalate situations. They are taught to respond to what is presented to them. This is what happens all too often with those in positions of power, like law enforcement. People won't automatically respect and listen. They will challenge those in authority. Then the back and forth ensues, and then we all know what ends up happening. It becomes a thing of I'm right, I have to win vs. I don't care if you think you're right, I have to win.

Now even though anger is unfortunately a major part of many relationships, it is not the fact that it exists as much as it is how it is used against the significant other in those relationships. For the longest of time, men have been the ones bestowed with the honor of being mean, overbearing, stubborn, unwilling to listen, you name it. But as of late, women have been attempting to take this title away and the way they seem to do it is by the way they talk to the significant other. You see when an individual gets angry; they have but a few choices as to their next course of action. They can keep that anger to themselves. They can express that anger in a healthy manner or they can (and this seems to be the one quickly gaining popularity) project their anger onto the other party. You see when an individual has pent up anger that he or she does not know how to properly release, he or she will release it to whomever is unfortunately in the vicinity. This can be kids, random individuals or the significant other. When it is the significant other, this individual will curse at him or her, verbally assault this individual and sometimes even lay hands on this person. It is not as common for women to physically assault men but the verbal abuse that men endure is allowed and accepted because women have this whole emotional title hanging over their heads and people will often mistakenly classify their actions as beyond their control. People are quick to say that women always argue and yell and scream. But this misdirected anger is many times what keeps couples from properly communicating with one another and the main reason is because the potential for the anger is what causes the fear of not wanting to talk. Think about it: if a man knows that a woman will get mad and start cursing him out if he says something that she may not like or may interpret the wrong way, then that man more than likely will not say anything to her. How is this a problem? Women love to talk. So if they are talking to the man who is restricting his conversation because he doesn't want to argue, the insistence will be seen as nagging on her part. One of two things will happen: the man will argue back or he will leave because he is in need of peace of mind. If a woman does not understand this she will be under the impression that the man is just trying to avoid her. But what this all too often is, is little more than a classic case of one person interpreting things other than the way they were intended. You see far too often, many women feel that everything they try to get across to men is helpful while on the other hand many men feel that they are intentionally trying to hurt them. Yes this boils down to communication, but this is also something, which should have been tackled in the beginning stages of the relationship. You see the problem that too many people in this world have is that they feel as long as there are no arguments in the relationship, then the relationship is going well. They feel that if they do argue, it is not a stepping stone to a better relationship. They feel that it is often a stepping stone to the end of the relationship. People try to avoid adversity as much as possible, instead of welcoming it and learning from it. And this is why relationships fail. If people would put restrictions and stipulations on how they allow others to talk to them, there would never be another argument in existence. If people would say 'I don't like this' in the beginning of relationships or if people would say 'I don't like what you did' and not a week after the fact but right then when the significant other has done the offending act, there would not be a chance for the significant other to talk down to the other because they would let the significant other know that that type of behavior is not going to be tolerated. But the problem that we have in relationships is that we allow things to go on that we do not like. This is so basic but at the same time so detrimental. If you don't want somebody to do something to you, don't let them do it. This includes how they express their anger and how they express their concern. What we are too often afraid of is losing the individual that we think is for us, our life partner. But here's the thing: if this person is really meant for you, then telling him or her the truth about what you want and expect in your relationship should bring him or her closer, not scare them away. And if by chance the truth does push the other away, he or she was not really meant for you anyway. When it comes to how individuals talk to one another, the igniters of unhappiness do not have to be anything major or ongoing. A certain response to a simple question is usually all it will take to upset the other party. An example of this is 'what do you want?' You see, some people in relationships will call the other on the phone and the other will respond in that manner. Some people will try to get the other's attention and he or she will respond in the same manner – and the responding party does not necessarily have to be upset to have that type of response leave their mouths. It is the fact of how it is received by the significant other, which causes the problem. Many in relationships talk a certain way. They speak aggressively. They speak rudely. They speak in a manner, which to them is a little assertive but to the one they are involved in a relationship with, disrespectful. And the problem with this is that the ones speaking this way do not understand. What I used to advise people who had to deal with this situation and those closely related, to do was the exact same thing to the significant other that he or she was doing to them. It was beneficial for a few. And the reason why was because the majority of the ones who were speaking in the disrespectful tone were so used to being disrespectful and disrespected that they did not know how their actions came across to other people and proof of this was when the significant other would say the exact same thing to the other, which was said to them, the other would respond with 'why are you talking to me like that?' or some variation. They would say 'this is me, this is how I talk.' But yet and still they would not approve of when it is done to them by someone else. People do not realize how this boils down to simple respect. The simple respect of 'give me the respect I give you and I will give you the respect you give me and life as we know it will be wonderful.' No. What some people do is say whatever the fuck comes out of their unfiltered little mouths and they don't focus on how it is received, until it comes back to bite them in the ass. Now what should be understood is that when you are by yourself, meaning single, you can say or do anything in this freaking world that you please. But for crying out loud, when you are in a relationship, you must think first before you say things, which may offend the significant other. The age old adage of do unto others as you would have them do unto you is one of the truest things, which should be adhered to in relationships. Think before you speak. Think before you do. It is the same as defensive driving. By yourself, you can drive as safe or reckless or as fast or crazy as you want to – but when you either have somebody in your car with you or you are on the road with other people, you have to think and act for their benefit. Instead of defensive driving, you can call this defensive relationshipping. If only people would think for the other party in the relationship first, I believe half of all problems in relationships would be eliminated. But you see, this is how misinterpretations have a severe impact on relationships. Somebody saying 'honey' and the other responding with 'what do you want?' will lead the first to believe that the other is mad or upset or simply has an attitude. And it is not so much that the words themselves are spoken as much as it is in the manner in which they are spoken. You see, the same phrase spoken with two different tones of pitch will give the impression that one time he or she is mad and the next he or she is not. And if the message of the significant other being mad or upset is received, what will more than likely happen is the one who thinks the other has the attitude will respond in defense mode or damage control mode. Aka 'what the fuck did I do?' Now there are other words, phrases and questions, which will effectively cause the other to feel a certain type of way when they are used. For instance, when it comes to questions, there is the all time favorite: are you fucking stupid or what? When it comes to simple words and phrases, there are: loser! And 'you will never be anything!'

Chapter

5

Trust Issues Are Not Always In Your Mind

One of the biggest challenges to a relationship, whether that relationship is professional or personal, is being able to completely trust the person you are in that relationship with. Many people will argue this logic because their present relationship has little to no adversity or reason to doubt the honesty and fidelity of the significant other. However I believe this to be because of two reasons. The first is because the relationship has yet to be challenged and the second is because it is not the significant other who causes the issue of distrust, it is the human being. Some people will say that it is beyond the human being. Some will say that it is spiritual. Who knows? To date, excluding religious entities and superheros, there has not been one person who falls under the umbrella of infallible. Nobody's perfect. Let me say this again; nobody in this world is perfect. What we far too often do is project that expectation or belief of perfection onto the significant other until the significant other smashes that belief by doing nothing more than being the person he or she was born to be. Proof of this is how at the beginning of relationships, everybody makes the same promises and vows and commitments only to let a few weeks, months or years go by and end up breaking them. To be perfect, the significant other must do everything, which is right in this world and must do everything that you like, meaning everything, which is right for you. There is no way both things are going to happen. You see, our mistaken interpretation of trust is unfairly projected onto the individual we are interested in even before we become involved in a relationship with him or her. And this is because everybody has a different interpretation of what trust is and everybody also has a different interpretation of what violations of that trust is as well. Our ability to trust is hampered by several things. The first is the understanding that we are all human and capable of failure. Let me say this again: there is no trust in relationships because there is no trust in the human being. Two, the instruction given from friends and family, three, reality show buffoonery and four, true life experience. Here's an example: if you grow up in a household, where you experience cheating firsthand, and by this I mean you see your mother sneaking random men into the apartment when your father is at work and when she thinks that you are sleep, how easy will it be for you to not only receive those flashbacks when you are older, but be led by those when the opportunity presents itself to trust or not trust the significant other? If as a child, your father takes you to the park and uses you to meet women, how easy will it be to believe the significant other will do the exact same when you are home cooking the family dinner or trying to get a break from your motherly duties? It will be very easy and the reason why is because the mind for some strange and uncanny reason will hold on to all of the negativity and ration out the good. And if any of you are thinking that these are extreme examples, you know like that doesn't really happen, then just think for a second how many times have you seen a woman walk up to a complete stranger who has a young child in his arms and initiate conversation. They will say things like 'omg, she's so cute!' or 'how adorable!' or something along those lines. Now just think if the young man was of a certain mindset and he refused to tell these women who approach him and the child about the mother at home. Or what if he said that he and the mother were divorced or he was widowed perhaps. Do you have any idea of how many women would throw themselves at the prospect of being involved with somebody who falls into the 'good man' status? Plenty. You see people manipulate situations for their own benefit all the time. It is the taking advantage of others, which this country is built on. It is also this taking advantage of situations mentality that you must be able to put aside in your relationship.

But here's the thing: you have to use common sense and actual knowledge of the significant other and what he or she has the propensity to do, to do so. This part is not that easy. When born, people know nothing. They have to be taught everything. They jump into relationships not knowing how to trust, then expect to pull that trust out of the air when necessary. It doesn't happen like that. You see, there are many trust building exercises that therapists use after infidelity has been a part of a relationship to help rebuild that relationship, but my question is, who teaches people how to trust the significant other before a relationship is initiated? The reason why this is a major problem is because the ones who are doing the teaching are all too often the ones who have been hurt, which basically boils down to them trying to teach trust from a place of distrust. Not an easy task. You see, what many parents do is teach trust by waiting until something either happens or doesn't happen and then say I can trust you or I can't. If nothing ever happens that will challenge trust, then trust is given. If trust is broken one time or many times, the parents will reason that trust is not deserved. And this is how the lesson of trust is taught and passed on. And this is also why trust is manipulated so easily. You see everybody says they know about deception but they for some reason or other feel that it will never apply to them or their relationship.

Many times in relationships people will say to the other, there is something about them that they don't trust. Now when it comes to relationships, it is a well known but highly debated fact that people look for perfection in their relationships. They expect the significant other to be perfect in all of his or her interactions and activities. They expect the significant other to be completely trustworthy. There are no ifs, ands or buts regarding this fact. But see here is the thing, which causes problems in relationships: I know you can't be perfect and I know you can't be completely trustworthy but I will accept you and be happy with you until you show me that you're not. You see everybody is going to mess up somewhere in a relationship. It is just the way life is. There is nobody in this world, who has been in a relationship and can say that he or she has never messed up or made a mistake. But even with this level of understanding, we expect not to see or experience the failure, which is sure to come. When it comes to being trustworthy, most times it is automatically assumed that an individual is trustworthy if he or she has done nothing to contradict that fact. You can send a person to the store and he or she will return with all of your change, then said individual is trustworthy.

You can let somebody hold your car and if they bring it back in one piece, then they too are trustworthy. But when people catch you in things, which shatter the trustworthiness, like lying or lying about an individual of the opposite sex, it may be years before that trust is returned. Now the interesting thing about the destruction of trust is that even if the trust is destroyed, whether by not yet dispelled suspicions or whether it has been destroyed by an actual occurrence, many people will still continue on in the relationship. I say this is interesting because most people reading this will agree that if there is no trust in a relationship, then there is no relationship. But as stated before there is still a relationship. So my question is how? This is the pacification technique many couples use, which is masqueraded as a real relationship. This 'relationship' is allowed to continue because the person who is not trusted is providing something that the other cannot do without or chooses not to do without and because the one who does not trust, is accepting the distrustful individual under the guise of well nobody's perfect, so I have to allow for some failures in the relationship. In other words, they are continuing on in a fake relationship because you cannot logically have a true relationship without trust but yet and still the two are still carrying on a relationship. You see this is why I say many relationships are more about necessity than love, or anything else for that matter. If an individual not knew, but actually believed in his or her heart that a relationship was about honesty and truthfulness and all that other good stuff, and this individual was not receiving any part of it, no matter how miniscule or insignificant, that individual would drop the relationship right then, and right there. But what happens all too often is we get tricked into this whole 'unconditional love' thing or this whole 'love will propel us through all types of adversity' thing and the next thing you know, we are stuck in a fake relationship, unsuccessfully trying to make it better. Now here's the thing with that: let's say that you are one of those rare people who are in search of total honesty and truth and justice and the American way and all that – and you leave your relationship because you are not receiving trust, the one thing, which you need to be able to call your relationship completely honest. It is a pretty good to excellent chance that much of society will disagree with your decision and possibly ridicule the hell out of you because now you do not have a relationship all because you wanted to find perfection. People will say nobody's perfect, so you have to allow for some failures in your relationship. In other words when you go looking for perfection, you will end up alone. This is the hypocrisy about relationships. You see, everybody I have ever met has told a lie at one time or another. It could have been a white lie, a lie to save their ass, a lie about why they were late for work, a lie to avoid a traffic ticket or a lie about infidelity. It could even be one of those lies that you don't actually speak; you know the deception by omission thing. But the bottom line is that there more than likely will be some kind of deception in your relationship because you are dealing with the human spirit - the faulty by nature and design human spirit. To have a relationship last, you will have to accept certain things. There is no getting past that. The only choice you have in that equation is how much you will choose to accept. You can never say don't ever lie to me because many times an individual's understanding of a situation is directly related to that individual's interpretation of that situation. So you may interpret something as a lie when in actuality it is something that you do not completely understand.

There is another thing, which contributes to trust, rather the lack of trust developing in a relationship. And this thing is called uncontrolled forces of nature. An example of this is if you and the significant other are apart from one another, and you call the significant other, who is home and he or she says that they are sleeping and you say okay go back to sleep, I'll call you later. And then on a different occasion, you call the significant other at home and he or she says that they are again sleeping, and the same thing happens, where you tell them that you will call back later. Now what will make an individual sit up and pay attention is when you call the significant other and he or she says that they were sleeping, but didn't answer the phone because they didn't hear it this time. Now sometimes a call can be placed and not received by the intended party. Sometimes the phone may fall off the bed and onto the floor. Sometimes any number of things could happen which are beyond our ability to control and which will cause a certain amount of doubt. This is what you must watch out for. You see, the average individual will say 'why is it that every other time I call you, you answer the phone but today, all of a sudden you didn't hear it?' Trust me when I tell you that I have been in this situation more times than I prefer to talk about. You see, sometimes a person in a relationship will fall asleep with the phone right next to him or her. And sometimes this person who may be a wild sleeper may toss and turn and unintentionally wrap the phone up in the blanket or sheet they are sleeping under, thereby muffling the sound to the point where it is not audible to the sleeping individual. Sometimes the person may fall asleep and forget to charge the phone, which will result in this person not answering the phone all night and sometimes the phone itself may be bought from one of those not anywhere near legitimate phone stores and they may have no warranty and may just fail at the exact moment you are trying to call. There is even the possibility that the phone company itself is having issues which will cause the call your significant other is expecting you to answer, to not go through. In the course of a relationship all of these things can happen. The funny thing about it is that often these things happen when couples are going through or are on the verge of adversity. This is why trust has to be at an all time high when you are in a relationship. Misunderstood situations, as what these are commonly called, have a very colorful history of being mistaken for infidelity.

If there were not trust issues with the human being, then the average person could play three card monte or any random variety street gambling game, win and be assured of safe travels home with all of the money that he or she has won. But how often does that happen? People have been known to get beat up and robbed, even worse, if the money, which was won, and more, was not given back. Every situation in life, as a matter of fact has been manipulated for criminal or violent activity. So how can anyone reasonably expect there to be complete trust in this world? With infidelity being one of the most trust destroying examples, more people should understand that there is obviously going to be hesitation and suspicion in regard to relationships. I mean there are relationships, which go on for years while an extra person is involved. Those in positions of power for example, have relationships with subordinates for years upon years and everything is fine until the subordinate wants something from the other besides sex. Then it becomes troublesome. Then it becomes violent. Then it becomes 'we were just fucking' on the part of one and 'I thought you loved me' on the part of the other. Then comes the outside involvement. The newspapers, the blackmail, the 'everything it should not have ever been had the relationship been based on something besides sex and lies and deception. People see this and they attribute that to either the downfall of society or the amount of distrust in their lives and or relationships – and people have the nerve to wonder why there is no trust.

When people have trust issues, they are based on personal experience more than hearsay. They see their parents and friends cheating on one another. They see cheating going on in almost every television show they watch. They see their best friends, some of whom they have known their entire lives, stealing from them or talking bad about them behind their backs. This is sad to say and it may be very debatable but I doubt seriously that the human being, the human spirit, is capable of complete honesty. And by this I mean that either you are going to be guilty in your mind or you are going to be guilty in your actions. For those who may disagree, tell me that you have never had a mean thought or a dirty thought or a thought, which was anything other than completely pure in your entire life. Sorry, not believing it. The only thing, which separates you from the bad people in this world, is whether you act on those bad thoughts or not. When somebody steps on your toe and doesn't apologize for doing so, the first thought is usually not to forgive. The second thought is. The first thought is to curse the inattentive or disrespectful son of a bitch out. When something happens that you know is going to get you in trouble, how many of you say 'oh hell, I'll just tell the truth and take my lumps' or do you say 'let me see if there is a way I can get out of this unscathed first?' You see, even if a person does not act on his or her thoughts, the thoughts are not always going to be pure. Only perfect people always have perfectly pure thoughts. How many of you reading this fall into the category of perfect? Now another reason trust issues are so prevalent is because people in relationships only divulge certain things to the significant other. They feel he or she doesn't need to know this or that. This is not lying. This is being deceptive by omission. The problem with this is that in a relationship, the one thing, which is expected but not always received, is total honesty. We expect the significant other to tell us everything about their lives. This includes from where they are, where they are going, and who they are with or going to see – all the way to what happened in your life before you met me, who did you date, did you do time? And so on and so on. What most people have a habit of doing is filtering out the bad so that individuals are only shown in a good light. This happens before the relationship is initiated, in the beginning stages of the relationship and in many cases, all throughout the relationship. The problem? If one significant other were to ask the other 'where were you today?' and the answer, which was received included everything but the fact that the significant other went to see the ex, then no matter what the reason for seeing the ex, the significant other will always be thought of as intentionally leaving out that bit of information because of something derogatory. Now the thing about this is that the derogatory belief does not have to be based on anything that the significant other has done. The overwhelming influence of society will many times make any left out information, no matter how miniscule and insignificant to the one who left it out, gigantic in nature to the one who finds out later that it was left out. You see this is what many interpret as hiding stuff. You think it doesn't mean anything so you don't say anything but I think it means everything and you are choosing to keep it from me, see the difference? Sometimes people do so many things in one day that they forget a few of the things they have done. A suspicious significant other may interpret that forgetting as intentional and will often accuse the other as being deceitful or trifling. This is why in addition to trusting others, an individual has to be able to forego the opinions and instruction from society and believe that people are human and not superhuman, and that they are capable of making honest mistakes, like forgetting. But we all know that people not only want perfection in a relationship, they expect and demand it. Men are famous for forgetting birthdays and anniversaries, and many women have grown to accept that but just let it be a situation of an individual not remembering what he or she did earlier today or yesterday for that matter and watch all hell break loose. In relationships, the significant other wants to be the go to person. He or she wants to know everything about what the significant other is feeling, dealing with or going through. If one significant other cannot trust the other to come to him or her before going to others outside of the relationship, he or she will feel that the other does not trust them and will not allow trust to grow between the two.

Blocked Numbers And Related Issues Of Distrust

The main reason this happens is because of distrust. It is distrust on either the part of the one calling or on the part of the one being called. What people in relationships do is go through many periods of adversity. Sometimes during these adversity filled periods, they wish not to speak to one another – or maybe one wants to and the other doesn't. What is common practice if one does not answer calls from the other, is to call from a private or blocked number. This is also protocol for those who are cheating. What people who are cheating many times do is save the numbers of the one or ones they are cheating with under a blocked name. In other words, if your name is Jeremiah, the person you are in a clandestine relationship with could have you listed in her phone as blocked, which means if you call, your number will show up as a blocked number. And what experienced perpetrators of infidelity will often do is say 'I don't know who that is and I don't answer blocked calls' thereby giving the significant other, who may be in close proximity, peace of mind and no reason to wonder about who is calling. When the significant other calls from a blocked number, it could be because the other is ignoring this person's calls or it could be because he or she, after hearing the above excuse, wants to see if the other will in fact answer a call from a private or blocked number. You should also be aware that when phone service is initiated, many times people are given the option to whether or not they wish their number to be displayed and there are some phone companies, which allow you to block your number for and from certain calls, so it is not always about deception.

When people have trust issues, they will do certain things to satisfy their curiosity while giving the significant other the belief that there aren't any trust issues at all. A popular for instance is what happens when people in relationships get on social media sites and stay on them for years and never post one status update. They do so just so that they can be the eyes and ears of their significant others' interactions. They will monitor their page and activities and be ever so quick to say who's that and why is he or she liking your pictures or why is this one always commenting on whatever you say and so on and so forth. But you see, this is often a reflection of the insecurity an individual has within himself. What many in this world do is project their behavior, actions and responses onto other people when it comes to infidelity. These people think 'I know how men think, I know how women think' and a good majority of the time how men and women think in their eyes is negative. It is negative because often they themselves are dirty or were dirty in their past. An unwillingness or inability to trust shows that in many cases, not all but in many, people are not able to be trusted themselves. People in relationships who do not trust one another will do things which mimic concern. They will call the significant other and if the significant other were to say that he or she is sleeping for example, then the other will call back soon there after from a blocked number and not for any valid reason except that of making sure that the other answers the phone and is actually sleeping. People who do not trust will make concern calls or calls for nothing just to say they care, three to four times back to back, in an effort to do nothing more than satisfy their curiosity about the other's actions and whereabouts.

Passwords And Phones

One of the biggest and most unnecessary arguments in relationships is the 'if you trust me, you should let me see your phone.' It is so unbelievably funny how people will swear up and down that they trust the significant other but will have a pass code on their phones, they won't let the significant other look through their phones or they will keep their phones on vibrate while in the presence of the significant other. Now the vibrate thing is debatable. Sometimes people work where they are not allowed to have cell phones so these people will put their phones on silent so as not to be disturbed or get in trouble during work. And sometimes these people forget to take the phone off silent when they get home and are around the significant other, so it could be a situation of an honest mistake. As far as not giving the combination to the pass code, that is something completely different. A password or pass code is utilized for secrecy. There are no two ways about that. In a relationship, there is no room for secrecy. Now there are many people who will say that you do not need to know every part of an individual's past. I believe this is because an individual has parts of his or her past that he or she is ashamed of or is because he or she does not completely trust the other person in the relationship. If there was nothing in the past to be ashamed of and or you trusted this individual completely, then you would feel comfortable enough to tell the other everything about your life and he or she would do the same and life as you both know it would be wonderful – but this is not the case. This is never the case. Some people in relationships are dirty. Some in relationships feel that a man should never know everything a woman does and some feel a woman should never know every move of a man. What this feeling is going to lead to is a whole lot of game play between the sexes. In other words, I am going to keep you at arms length just because as a man or woman, I am supposed to. You see, the thing that people have a hard time understanding is that relationships are <u>full</u> of deception and misunderstood situations. If you for instance call your ex boyfriend or ex girlfriend but don't tell the significant other about it, nine times out of ten, the suspicious nature of the significant other will take hold and guide the significant other's thinking. They will ask why are you calling but more than likely, they will already have an answer made up in their mind as to what the conversation was about – and no matter what you say, the answer they have in their minds will not be a positive one. There is also the 'who is this person and why is he or she calling you or why are you calling him or her?' Here's the thing: no matter what you do, you will never be able to talk about everything and everybody you come in contact with. You may call somebody by mistake. Somebody may call you by mistake. If you have the type of significant other who believes little to nothing, especially when it comes to situations he or she doesn't completely understand, the above situation may make him or her go completely off the deep end. So sometimes not showing the significant other your phone could be seen as a preventative measure to save your sanity. But this is one more of those reasons why you should know somebody before you get involved with that somebody, as well as his or her reactions to certain stimuli. Sometimes people over react to certain misunderstood situations and this is why others resort to covert countermeasures like hiding phone numbers or not allowing the other access. It is not always because the other is doing something bad. Many times it is but not always. You see, having a password, which you will not relinquish, is the equivalent of saying 'I don't want you in my business.' Now here's the thing about that: when in a relationship, the business of one, <u>automatically becomes the business of the other.</u> When you restrict any part of it, whether by not speaking or by not sharing passwords or by not letting the other see your phone, you will be seen as the one bringing detriment and unnecessary drama to the relationship. So the bottom line all comes down to a choice. Am I to be completely truthful and at the same time allow myself to be completely vulnerable? Or do I restrict certain parts of my existence as a form of protecting my self, while at the same time, making you think I am being dishonest?

Temptation

Many people in relationships have never experienced temptation but yet the ones they are involved in the relationship with will expect that they know how to not only handle being tempted but successfully circumvent that temptation as well. Now this is an exceptionally tall order for some people and the reason why is because for people to be able to respond or react positively to a situation, they more than likely have to have some kind of experience of being placed in that situation. Case in point: some people from well populated areas will go to less densely populated areas to find husbands or wives. Some of the people from the densely populated areas are used to seeing and being around maybe millions upon millions of people in their lifetime while those from the opposite side of the spectrum may come from a country or part of the world where they see and come in contact with no more than three to five thousand people in a lifetime. Now let's say that someone goes to one of the less populated areas and finds a significant other and brings this individual back to wherever they call home. This individual may get approached in a month by the amount of people who are equivalent to what this person is used to seeing in a year. And not only that, the caliber of individuals who approach the significant other may be ten times better looking than what the significant other is used to. My question is this: can blame really be afforded to the significant other if he or she has never been tested with this volume or caliber of temptation? You see some people are not used to the game, which is prevalent in some parts of the world. Some people believe everything, which is told to them and this is why certain people will tell somebody they have no intention of doing anything besides sleeping with, that they are in love with this person after knowing them for all of two weeks. The reason why is because they will believe it. It is because they believe in the good of man. To excel in anything in this world, you need practice. This includes relationships and this especially includes how to resist temptation in relationships. Now temptation does not even have to be a thing of massive geographic proportions. Individuals can live in the same town, on the same street or in the same building and be detrimentally tempted to cheat on the significant other. You see, the way this world is, with jobs draining the lifeblood out of you, with children's demands for time and attention, minimizing the quality time between you and the significant other and countless other seemingly unavoidable interruptions, sex between a committed couple can seem like an impossible quest. It may be even almost impossible for committed couples to see one another enough to make plans for quality time and this is where the opportunity for temptation is at its greatest. You see, the one thing that people in relationships have to realize is that there will ALWAYS be those attempting to intercede their way into your relationship. People will ask all the time 'how's your relationship going?' or 'how's your significant other?' And they will watch like a hawk to make sure that whatever you say, your actions match. If they watch you and do not see you spending time with the significant other, you best believe they will fathom that you and the significant other are not happy – and because of this belief, they will try to make an unwelcome move on your relationship. Some bad people will think on a totally different level. They will see that you are happy with the significant other and <u>still</u> try to make an unwelcome move on the relationship because they may think that they will be a better fit for either you or the significant other. In a relationship, there are two words you should always remember and live by if you want your relationship to continue. Trust nobody.

Misinterpretation

The way that many relationships are set up nowadays is to always make the woman seem like she is less important than the man. So consequently, the man will always have to be taking care of her. And this is even if the woman doesn't need to be taken care of. The perception by the world at large is that a man has to take care of a woman, period. If a man is not doing what is historically accepted and expected by others, then he will be accused of not being a man. This is why there is so much hypocrisy and distrust in relationships. Women can make and keep their money totally separate and hidden from the man they are involved with – and still ask for and receive more from the man they are involved with simply because they are women, and the perception of society will be completely on their side. Add the fact that probably every other man walking the face of the earth will think that if a woman ever says she is in need, his moral obligation will dictate that he be right there to help, just because he thinks that she cannot do it herself, you know because of the ole woman are the lesser, weaker sex thing. This will also make any man who gives assistance to a woman in a relationship, think that the man she is with is not providing for her the way he should. Otherwise she would not be going to the next man for help. This will lead to the thought that there is some sort of adversity in the relationship, which will lead to the thought that the man giving assistance will make a better fit for the woman who is in need. This will also make the man in the relationship believe that the woman has some type of interest in the man giving assistance, which is not exactly platonic. And this as we all know will eventually lead to suspicions about infidelity, which will lead to arguments about infidelity, which will more than not, eventually lead to infidelity. You see anytime anyone has to go outside of their relationship for help from the opposite sex, the thought will be that it is because of a physical desire. The thought will be 'you are coming to me because you are not happy in your relationship, you are not sustained in your relationship, or you are not satisfied in your relationship.' People will say it is not always like that and the above examples are isolated cases but it is like that. This is the way people think. If people did not think like this, then the divorce rate would not be as high as it is. If people did not think like this, then they would not be so eager to offer sex when an individual in a relationship is in need of financial help or nothing more than someone of the opposite sex to give a male or female perspective. If people did not think like this, then they would not be so quick to cheat, while basing their actions on not proof, but only the belief that the other has done or is doing something wrong.

The unfortunate truth surrounding some relationships is that some women will feel that the man they are in a relationship with is not being a man if he cannot provide her with all of her worldly desires. Some women will say 'you are not a man because a man has money.' 'A man takes care of his woman' and things of that nature. Now none of this is most likely true but it is that the man in her life is not living up to her interpretation of her ideal man. And this is one of the things that will cause the relationship to have unnecessary problems. This is one of the things, which should have been discussed in the beginning of the relationship – not that the woman has expensive tastes but how she will act if her expensive tastes are not met and will the man even be able to provide them. You see what people all too often do is assume that once the relationship has started, then everything which is supposed to happen to ensure the relationship will go the way it is supposed to go, will automatically happen as well. The man will always have the amount of money the woman needs. The woman will always be attractive and receptive to the man. The attention, which is shared between the couple at the beginning of the relationship, will always be shared all throughout the relationship and so on. But it doesn't happen like that. Relationships are preparation for the inevitable. The inevitable is negativity and problems and promises, which are no longer able to be met. And even if the inevitable does not happen, couples still should be prepared in case it does.

Old Friends And New Relationships

One of the things, which have always given a problem in relationships, has been this thing of trusting the significant other around the opposite sex when he or she is alone. What people all too often and mistakenly do once they get involved, is go cold turkey in regard to friends, and while I sincerely believe certain friends should be kept at a distance, some friends should not be hidden and long term friends should not be excluded. The problem is that there is little to no trust in relationships and this is why the general consensus states that a married individual cannot just go and hang out with an unmarried friend, even if they have been friends an entire lifetime. Even if there is trust in the relationship, the fact that others who do not have the same level of trust, are either involved in the relationship or close to the relationship, they will many times add their two cents to the effect of 'you're letting your wife go out with another man? And vice versa. You see, the bottom line is or should be this: either you trust the significant other or you don't. Either you trust the significant other not to violate the vows and boundaries of your relationship or you don't. And my thing is if you do not trust this individual, the reasons why you became involved or committed, must really be re examined. The thinking of society will determine that before you get married you are allowed to date anybody you want, as well as hang out with as many friends as possible. The rules of society further dictate that if you are dating someone particular or steady, then you cannot date anyone else at the same time, but the two of you can still go out with friends, either together or alone. Now the controversial part about the whole dating relationship thing is that once you get married or become strongly committed, then you are no longer allowed to hang out with members of the opposite sex, even if they were friends before the marriage took place. And this is because when friends hang out, there is almost always an element of sexual tension in the group. Either one of the guys wants to screw one or all of the girls or one of the girls wants to screw one or all of the guys, secretly of course. Now in the general overview of things, it will seem like just a bunch of good friends spending quality time together but look closer and you will see that everybody has an agenda – and here's the thing: the agenda does not die. Guys know this and girls know this as well. This is why guys will say 'I don't want you hanging around with that guy because I know how guys are, I know what he is thinking' or girls will say 'I know she wants you.' This thinking occurs, even if these people are friends. This thinking will resonate in the mind of the significant other because they will more than likely know many of the things that you will never be shown by the friend of the significant other, until of course the two of you are somewhere alone and out of the blue he or she makes a completely inappropriate comment about sex or about the man or woman you are involved with in the hopes that he or she can use whatever your response is to eventually begin a sexual relationship or a regular relationship. What many ignorant and unknowing people will do is say things to the effect of 'that's your friend, he or she would never think like that' or 'he or she would never try something like that' but here's the thing: People will. The main reason deception is allowed to not only exist in this world but prevail, is because deception does not say 'hi I'm deception.' Deception never shows its head until it's too late. Now for those of you who may not know, the best way to prevent infidelity or those situations, which resemble infidelity, is to not allow yourself to be placed in those situations in the first place. If you never hang out with friends of the opposite sex, then there will never be reason for the significant other to believe that one, you are doing something dirty and two, that you were ever even tempted. Now granted, this is obviously a ginormous show of distrust on the part of the significant other but many times in relationships you have to do what will put the mind of the significant other at ease so that your mind can rest peacefully as well. The controversial thing about this is if a person tries to restrict any part of your freedom, then he or she is controlling you. Relationships are not about control. They are about each party in the relationship having the freedom to do whatever he or she pleases as long as it does not upset the other party. If an individual says I don't want you to see this particular individual because of whatever reason and you go, the thought will be that you disrespected the relationship by not respecting the wishes of the significant other. So many times it becomes a situation of give up my friends, whom you don't like to please you or keep my friends, whom I like, to please me. A real conundrum, isn't it?

Chapter

6

Inconsistencies And Imitations Of Love

When it comes to love, people desire more than anything else, longevity and equality. They want the love or idea they have of love to not only be shared equally by the one they involve themselves with but for it to be shared for as long as humanely possible. This is an all too common expectation. But you see, what many relationships are, besides a whole bunch of expectation, is a whole bunch of imitation. They are the doing what mom has done or not done by a daughter and they are the doing what dad has done or not done by a son. They are the copying of what has been shown to them by those either in the public eye, such as reality show actors and actresses, or by friends and associates who have been together for seemingly eons. (The longevity factor.) Now the reason this is so common is because most people ironically do not plan for anything when it comes to relationships. They will plan for a vacation. They will plan for a wedding. They will plan for a hurricane or a tornado but just let it be something, which will pretty much change the course of their lives and what do they do? They say 'fuck it, let's just throw caution to the wind and ride this shit out.' Then, when problems start to creep into the relationship, as they surely will, the couples start to ask the ones who were being copied, for assistance. They start asking questions like 'why does a man do this or why does a man act like this?' 'Why does a woman get an attitude over something I think is miniscule?' And so on and so forth. They ask these things after the fact and of the wrong people and then wonder why their relationships suffer. Now understand, imitation is not always a bad thing. Most things in life are done because of imitation. In fact, it has often been stated that imitation is the most sincere form of flattery. In other words, I am going to copy you because I like and admire what you are doing. Nobody in this world knows everything necessary to either initiate or continue a relationship without some sort of tutelage. People have to base their interpretation of a relationship on someone or something. The problem is that too many people base their relationships on the wrong thing. Just because people are together for many years and they do not try and kill each other, does not mean they are completely happy in their relationship. Just because people are related or parental figures or actual parents, does not mean they make the ideal role models either. People have to follow the right teachers to have their relationships last but the thing about finding the right teachers is that you will have to spend much of your lifetime trying to find out whose relationship will last the way you want yours to go. Now the copying of a relationship of someone you admire should be nothing more than a foundation on which to build. Parents who have been together for years and have raised successful children would be considered a good foundation. A good start. However, many times these people are less than completely happy. You see some people physically abuse their children or the ones they are in relationships with and the children still become financially successful or the relationship continues for fifty years. But is this the ideal thing to emulate? I believe not. People have to look much deeper than the surface when it comes to copying the 'ideal' family or individual. Relationships are imitated in many ways. They are inconsistent in mainly two. The first way is in thoughts and the second is in actions. When it comes to thoughts, one min they love you, the next it seems they don't. When it comes to actions, one minute they wanna marry you, the next minute they don't.

Many people, especially those in professional positions will say that the inconsistency in relationships in regard to love, comes from childhood. They say that many of the parents who had to earn a living for the family, had to leave the child alone and because of that fact, there are gaps in the attention and affection. This is somewhat understandable but my thing is if this were completely true, then wouldn't everybody in the world have issues with inconsistent behavior regarding love and relationships, because unless I am mistaken, no parent in the world has spent every waking moment with their son or daughter. Now true, I believe that inconsistent behavior stems from what a child may see, but more so from what a child is taught in regard to other people. You see people are not taught that love never takes breaks. It's not I love you until you piss me off – it's I love you period. But what people all too often do is live in the moment. If I'm happy now, then everybody is happy. If I'm not happy with you then bye – or at least bye until you decide to beg me to come back and I accept. This starts the back and forth, inconsistent type of relationship that confuses the fuck out of people. People are taught that it is okay to be indecisive when it comes to their relationships. People are taught that they don't have to call back when the significant other upsets them, and this is even if the significant other is unaware that he or she has made the other upset. People in relationships behave in inconsistent manners because often the level of interest in the relationship is not shared equally between both individuals in the relationship. When people are unhappy with one another or if they have passed that level of concern to where they do not care about the other and are just remaining in the relationship, they will do what is necessary but only when it is necessary. They will never make the needs of the other paramount, as what should be done in a normal relationship.

That Annoying Fucking Ex

One of the most severe threats to an individual's happiness in a relationship is the premature ending of that relationship. By premature, I am speaking of any reason for the relationship ending other than death. When most people get involved in relationships, they do not expect that the relationship they have will end due to unhappiness or infidelity or any garden variety reason. In fact the relationship expectation protocol states that if a relationship begins, then it will continue period. But as society too often shows, the only thing guaranteed to keep a relationship together is if both people want to stay together more than anything else. Unfortunately people who get into relationships do so for a myriad of reasons. Love is only one of those reasons. Some of them get together because the person they are interested in has a big behind. Some people get involved in a relationship because the one they are interested in has a big wallet. Then there are those who get involved because they desire children. And then there are those who have children but who also have no idea on how to properly care for those children, so they get involved with someone who fits the bill as far as what they deem a good caretaker to be. Now these people, who get involved with others for reasons which are not of the purest kind of criteria, are bad enough but there is another big thing, which threatens a relationship also, and this is what happens after one relationship ends and another one is initiated. An ex lover, more commonly referred to as an ex, will be created.

Now one of the many unsettling things about a new relationship, besides the getting to know stage, is the fact that the ex lover may decide to linger around. He or she may be the type who is slow to learn that the relationship is actually over. What is even worse, and what can be a severe detriment to the happiness of the new relationship is the fact that the new person in the relationship will more than likely have to deal with the ex as well. Often, as stated above, the fact that the partner in the new relationship has not completely cut off all ties with the ex, he or she may be giving the impression that there is a reason for the ex to hang around. By being 'friends' and still giving this individual the time of day, time will be taken from the new relationship and this will be seen as consistent attention not being paid to the new relationship.

The thing about the ex, which is not always understood, is that sometimes his or her interference is not always one sided. Sometimes the feelings from the previous relationship never really dies, and sometimes the feelings from the previous relationship are stronger than the ones in the new relationship. I mean who hasn't heard of an extended break, where a couple calls it quits, goes their separate ways and then a few weeks or months later, gets back together? Often while these individuals are in the midst of their 'unintentional' separation, they will date other people and will act or appear to be as happy as before the break up. Yet many times this is a ruse perpetrated on society at large, as well as on the new significant other. These new people are 'fillers' of space until the previous relationship manages to mend itself back together. Now sometimes it is not a ruse. Sometimes the relationship is actually over in the eyes of one but not in the eyes of the other. The unfortunate thought process of some people in this world resembles this: if you marry, then you are married for life, not until you tire of one another. The thought process is extended to include that since you are married or have been married one time, every other individual whom you may deal with, copulate with or marry after the fact will be nothing more than a temporary boyfriend or girlfriend. In addition to that, these people will use that belief to stay in close contact or close by in case the new relationship goes through a little too much adversity or the significant other has a change of heart.

Here's some often overlooked food for thought: once you fuck somebody and have a child with that somebody, you have given this person the pass to be in your life forever. People do not think about this beforehand. Many people who do not have kids may not see the potential agony in this statement. Many of them may feel it's okay, I love this person, and I will love him or her forever, and I will love the child we create together, forever. What they do not always realize is that people change. People change. People fucking change. In addition to this, these people many times do not focus on the fact that maybe the one they have decided to have a child with was not fully and completely known beforehand. And now that the relationship is experiencing adversity, the parent of the child, who has proven himself or herself very much unstable, desires to be in the life of not only the child but yours as well. Since you may fear for your child's safety or are concerned that being alone with the ex may not be in the child's best interest, you decide to keep in contact. Some people feel that if they can't have you, then nobody will. Some people feel that the only way a child can be properly taken care of is with the two original parents. When you break up with somebody, often the above two scenarios pop into play and with no advance warning. Scary isn't it? I truly believe that one of the most difficult things to find in this world nowadays is an uncorrupted person when it comes to a relationship. And by uncorrupted, I am not talking about mental issue having or diseased or even handicapped. I am talking about those who have no relationship past. I am talking about those who have never been married, never had a boyfriend or girlfriend, nothing. Totally untouched. The reason finding someone who falls into that sector is so difficult is because society puts so much pressure and emphasis on finding a significant other that by the time people are in elementary school, most of them have already had at least one failed relationship. Now this is bad, but this is not the worst thing that can happen to a relationship. The worst thing that can happen to a failed relationship is the fact that as mentioned before, it will create an ex. And what's even worse than just having an ex, is when that ex doesn't understand the relationship is actually over or they don't want to accept that the relationship is actually over. This is what will create a significant problem for you and everyone you decide to involve yourself with from the point of the break up on to infinity. The reason this becomes such a problem is because of the basics. The initial ground rules about the before, during and after of the relationship, must be cemented in the consciousness of the significant other at the beginning of the relationship. To avoid stalkers or the stalker mentality, you cannot have an amicable after the break up relationship, because the new individual in your life will not only believe that he or she will have the same type of interaction with you but will come to expect and demand it. When people see you still calling your ex and conversing with this individual, they will think that you are always going to be a nice person and if we break up after our relationship you will be just as nice to me. This thought process often stretches to if he or she is being nice to me, then maybe I can parlay that niceness into reconciliation. Yes, people think like that – and this is exactly why you have to be mean, even if it is totally uncharacteristic of you, after the relationship is over. Now here's what will happen if you are not mean: people will take your kindness for weakness. They call just to say hi, and make sure you're doing okay or to see if you need something, which they are more than willing to provide. They will start dropping by unannounced, for the above stated reasons and more. They start to hinder your chances at having either a new relationship or having a happy new relationship. You see sometimes this is done unintentionally, meaning an ex will linger around the new relationship because the feelings are still there and the old significant other is not mean (there goes that word again) enough to tell him or her to back the fuck off. Other times it is done intentionally because the ex wants back in to the relationship and is challenging the new lover to see what, if anything he or she will do to remove him or her from the equation. This will cause massive problems in the new relationship, especially if there is a child or children involved. The reason is having a child will be the perfect cover for this individual to be in close contact with the ex. And it could all be done under the guise of 'I'm just making sure my child is being taken care of.' Now on one side of the spectrum, this is probably the most noble thing you could do – making sure that no harm or foul comes to your child even though you are no longer in the relationship. On the other hand, this is player protocol – make the new partner in the relationship believe that you are solely interested in the positive raising of your child while your intentions are nothing more than bumping him or her out of the way so that you can weasel your way back into the relationship. Now how it will cause problems: nice people will not usually say 'leave me the fuck alone!' That's why they are called nice. They will say things like 'my new boyfriend doesn't want you hanging around.' To which the ex will more than likely respond with 'fuck that motherfucker.' This will cause an altercation between the ex and the new partner and the significant other will more than likely be in the middle trying to play peacekeeper. Since the ex will more than likely not want to give up so easily, and more than likely has nothing else to do than mess up the relationship between the new partner and his ex, he or she will involve himself or herself in the affairs of the new couple at any given chance and since the significant other is more than likely a nice individual, he or she will be thought of as still having a flame for the ex because he or she has not completely cut the other off. Now some of you reading this may wonder, am I instructing you to be an asshole when it comes to your ex just so that he or she gets the message of you not wanting to be bothered? The answer to that is a resounding fucking yes! You cannot call this individual just to see how he or she is doing. You cannot say I want to make sure that he or she does not do something to hurt themselves. Fuck 'em! <u>People need harshness in this world.</u> They need to understand that there will be ramifications, sometimes swift and severe ramifications, if they commit certain infractions. They need to know these things so that they will not commit certain infractions. They need to know this so that there will be no mistake about there being any chance for reconciliation. Ex. boyfriends and ex girlfriends who don't get the message will often think that they are still the main ones in the relationship. They will think in their twisted logic that the new boyfriend or girlfriend is the one infringing on their relationship – and with this twisted thinking, they will sometimes seek to do harm to the new significant other or the relationship. I mean have we not heard about this countless times on the news, on the television, radio and Internet about infidelity or suspected infidelity? Have we not heard far too many times about a jilted or jealous lover seeking to exact revenge on the partner who cheated or who was thought to be cheating? Many times this is little more than people who don't know their place, over reacting to a situation, which they don't completely understand. Exes have a long and varied history of not wanting to let go when a relationship has run its course. They figure that the other is just mad and will come around to the thinking of the other once he or she gets over being mad. And this is one of the main reasons why once a relationship is over, sometimes the best thing is complete resistance when it comes to seeing or wanting to see the other party. Sometimes you may have to relocate, even if only temporarily, because many people are raised to believe in the persistence overcomes resistance theory. In other words, the more they hound you, pressure you, call you, email you, etc. the more you will be inclined to respond. <u>And once you respond, it will be one step closer to them wiggling their trifling ass back into your life.</u> Is this what you want? Of course not. If you did want them in your life, you more than likely would not have let them get away in the first place. When it comes to kids, some people are master manipulators and they will use the unintentional assistance from the children, which were had during the relationship. They may know in their heart that you cannot stand the fucking air they breathe but you love your kids to death. So what these master manipulators may do is be as nice as they can to the kids, make the kids think that they are the best thing that God has created, spoil the kids freaking rotten so that as the relationship between you and him or her gets progressively worse, the relationship between them and the kids gets progressively better. This is done so that when you finally reach your breaking point and put this dirty mother fucker or trifling bitch out of your home and your life, the excessive amount of spoiling and affection, which was shown to the children will start to weigh on their precious little ignorant heads and they will start with the ever popular and annoying 'where's mommy?' 'Where's daddy?' 'I want mommy!' 'I want daddy!' And then you, if you have any heart in your body, will feel like a fucking heel if you keep your child away from their other parent. This is a fucking trick and I caution you don't fall for it. Kids are the best unintentional messengers in the world. A parent will say something to the effect of 'I love your mommy but she doesn't love me' and the next thing you know, while the mother and child are sitting down watching an episode of barney and friends, you know when they start singing that annoying ass I love you, you love me, the child out of the blue comes at you with 'mommy, why don't you love daddy anymore? And while you are sitting there dumbfounded trying to figure out where in the fuck did your precious bundle of joy get that from, while simultaneously trying to think of a way not to make the child's mother or father seem like the no good, dirty manipulative bastard that he or she is, they are more than likely somewhere smiling their ass off, playing the victim role. Quite often people bring this whole overbearing and annoying ex thing upon themselves and they do it by how the relationship starts. You see too many people have this blue lagoon, Romeo and Juliet belief of I will love you forever, which is projected onto any relationship that they seem to involve themselves in. They say things to the effect of 'when I love somebody, I love hard' or 'I don't do quickness. When I get into a relationship, it will be for the long term.' Often they say these things as a precursor to the relationship before they actually get to know the individual they are saying these things to. Then what happens is the individual who hears this, believes that just because he or she is chosen, the relationship will automatically be one, which is slated to last forever. This person will not for one second believe that maybe he or she is not the right one for the relationship and if the relationship ever goes awry, this person's thinking will revert back to the beginning of the relationship to where the other has recited the words above 'I'm in this for the long term and things of that nature.'

What people have to realize and remember is that they are not just dealing with a man or woman when they involve themselves in relationships. They are dealing with the historical representations of that man or woman. It is just like the thing with racism. People do not hate you because unless I am mistaken, it is pretty close to impossible to hate somebody who one, you have never met or interacted with and two, whom you know nothing about. When it comes to the relationship thing; people who involve themselves with you already have an idea of you before they even say hi to you. They already know how you are supposed to behave – even if you don't. And see this is why the getting to know aspect of any relationship is the most important. It is the time in which fantasies and illusions of the significant other are dispelled or solidified. This is the time when clarification of the all women are supposed to cook every night with a big meal on Sundays is necessary. This is the time when the belief that all men are supposed to be loving or caring or overwhelmingly dominant is supposed to be understood or challenged. But people do not do this. People are conditioned almost instinctively to respond in a reactive manner when it comes to most things in their relationships. They wait until things, which threaten the relationship occur and then they try and fix them. They are led by their we'll get to it when it happens philosophy and then we will worry about fixing it. This is the same thing as going with the flow. When you go with the flow, there is no direction in the relationship. Wait, actually there is. It is the direction the relationship wants to go. Dead fish go with the flow. It is not the direction that you or your partner wants. This is also the same thing as a fake relationship. What people in relationships often do is fail in the attempt to correct things, which are not conducive to the happiness of the relationship. They try talking to the significant other over and over and the significant other may not understand the problem or agree with the proposed solutions to the problem, whether by not being able to, or whether by not wanting to, and what happens is the other begins to feel that it is just easier to accept things the way they are instead of continually searching for a solution or fighting a losing battle. This is how you sometimes have what was described above as fake relationships. This is a prime example of what I spoke about elsewhere in regard to people becoming distant. You see if a person doesn't believe or was never taught that adversity is not a one time thing, that person may, after a big fight or after a trust challenging experience, believe that he or she is no longer in love – and he or she will base those feelings on the reactions of the other. You see if a person does not understand that love, and the steps leading up to it, is the equivalent of a recurring process, they may prematurely end a relationship because they don't know any better. Now the thing about this falling out of love thing is that people will not too much tell the other that they no longer love him or her. What they will do however is act the part. They will continue to let you believe they are still in love but may just be going through things, which they do not feel like sharing. Many people not only believe in but live by persistence overcomes resistance and because of that fact, they will become fucking intolerable to the ex. They will pester, perturb or just piss the other the fuck off in the hopes that old feelings will be rekindled and the relationship can either start anew or pick up where it left off. But what all too often happens is the other has made it up in his or her mind that there is no room for reconciliation but at the same time, the other does need peace of mind. So what more than likely will happen is the 'I'll take you back just to stop you from bothering me.' This does not mean that love has been in any way rekindled. This does not even mean that the prospect of love will ever be thought about on the rekindling scale. Now what a lot of people will do is make the ex believe that his or her interference is welcomed and they do this by not shutting the door relationship wise completely. They are always nice. They say things like you will always be in my heart and such. They never completely 'end' it. There is always an open. So the ex will logically think that because it was never stated I never want to see you or be bothered with you again, that there will always be a chance for reconciliation. This is the bullshit which many times makes it seem like infidelity is going on and what many times causes problems between the old partner and the new one. People have to set boundaries. This is not a one time thing. Boundaries must be set before the relationship is in place, while it is in place and especially after the relationship has ended so that the ex will know, which lines he or she can cross and which lines he or she cannot. But the problem is that many times people are too nice. They don't want to hurt the feelings of the ex. They know the ex is crazy so they don't want to make him or her violent. But doesn't all of this go back to the getting to know stage in the relationship? If you know the person you are getting involved with or contemplating getting involved with has fucking issues, why in the hell would you get involved in the first place??

The annoying fucking ex will make his or her presence known in every medium possible, especially on social media. He or she will like every post or tweet or whatever, which is uploaded by the former lover and many times this is done because of no reason other than to make the new lover jealous and cause issues between the two. In rare cases, the ex still carries a flame for the former and he or she will do everything to let it be known that the flame is still there. To counter this, the best advice, which can be given, is total and unrestricted avoidance of the ex significant other. You see sometimes the ex will not be capable of understanding that no means no. What this fool will do is cause detriment because as stated above, a flame is still held in the hopes of being rekindled or plain and simply, this dumb motherfucker has nothing else to fucking do. In either case, you have to be the one to prevent him or her from even having a chance to mess up your happiness or your potential long term happiness.

The Bullshit About 50/50

In a relationship there are always going to be expectations. These expectations are often justified and sometimes they are just way off the chart of sense and sensibility. They come before the relationship commences and they come after the relationship is underway. The thing about expectations is that no matter what, you cannot escape them. Now with that being said, for the longest of time, there has been this relationship ending expectation of 50/50. This is the belief that the relationship is comprised of a whole, aka 100% and both parties equal 50%. So that when both parties come together, the two halves will become one and both will total 100% aka a whole, complete relationship. Another interpretation of this belief is that everything which is done in the relationship must be completely equal, meaning if I do something then you must do something on the exact same level so that neither party will be in any way indebted to the other. This means that if I give you one hundred dollars just because you say 'sweetie, can I have a hundred dollars?' then when sweetie gets his or her paycheck, he or she will have to give that one hundred dollars back. This brings

154

up another dilemma. What happens if sweetie wants to buy something for the other? Does the other have to know the exact price so that he or she can appropriately reciprocate? What about when sweetie buys a gift for the other? Does the significant other have to buy a gift which costs the same or about the same amount of money? This brings up even another dilemma. If one party in the relationship makes much more than the other, then the other will obviously only be able to afford a certain amount of merchandise. Which means the two will never be on the same level financially, so from the start they will never be 50/50. This will open up a whole Pandora's box of questions and opinions from bff's and girlfriends and outsiders to the effect of 'if they not doing anything for you or if they are never buying you shit, then why are you with them?

CHAPTER

7

Only The Crazy Survive

The relationship. The pursuit of which defines some people's very reason for existing. It is the thought of not only finding but growing a relationship into a family for generations upon generations, which make some people forgo common sense and sensibility. It is the pursuit of finding what many deem the ultimate happiness in life. After exploring all of the potential positives of finding the right one, the Mr. or Miss. Right, there could only be one reason for shying away from the idea of a relationship, and that reason is because of the realization that many people walking the face of this earth are crazy as shit.

When it comes to getting involved in relationships, there are many popular sayings, which have been left behind from scholars, parents and those who have been on both, the good and bad sides of a relationship. One of those popular sayings is that a person has to be crazy to want to actually be involved in a relationship. There is another popular saying about relationships, which goes psycho sex is the best sex. And there is still yet another saying, which is also quite popular, that goes 'the relationship between a husband and wife is psychological. One is psycho and the other is logical.' I will leave it up to you, the general public to decide which one is which. Now when it comes to labeling an individual as being crazy behind the thought of wanting to become involved in a relationship, one just has to look at the preponderance of failed relationships and lunacy, which people who are still in relationships, have to deal with. And when you sit down and take stock of all the things, which are enjoyed by those on the single end of the spectrum vs. the things given up by those on the other end who are in relationships, there might actually be some validity to this belief. You see, people in relationships have to in essence, pull off the most difficult trick in the world. That trick is making a relationship work with somebody they do not know. Scratch all the nonsense about getting involved with a best friend or whomever you may actually believe is your soul mate or whatever because the bottom line is this; the only person you know or can know everything about in this world, is yourself. When you talk about some of the things, which fall under the lunacy category, there is the fact that many murder-suicides occur in what were once love filled relationships. Yes, people will, sometimes for nothing more than the mistaken belief that the significant other is doing or has done wrong, kill them and then kill themselves. Is this crazy? Of course it is. But here's the thing: <u>the individuals who commit these acts are rarely crazy.</u> The circumstances surrounding the unfortunate situation, are what are crazy. What a lack of understanding, combined with an all too common lack of communication will do, is many times make people act completely out of character, or out of the character that people have known them to have.

You have people cheating and committing all types of inappropriate behavior against one another because they are under the impression that the other has done something wrong. You have people going through phones and wallets and purses, all in an attempt to find evidence of unsavory behavior. You have law enforcement being called on significant others at all times of the night, as well as orders of protection being filed against one another because of violence or because of the threat of violence. Again, these people are not crazy. The circumstances surrounding the behavior are what are crazy. Now here's the really crazy thing: these people continue on in the relationship, talking about the above are just some of the 'bad' parts of a normal relationship.

Now there are considerable amounts of freedoms and luxuries, which are surrendered because of the transference from single to committed. And the problem with giving these things up is that those who do give them up are often completely unaware of the long term effects of parting with these freedoms and luxuries. The biggest freedom and luxury is the one of peace of mind. You will never have an argument with yourself, unless you are legitimately crazy. And this is a perk that money can never buy. There is the invaluable ability to get up and go anywhere you damned well please, at any time you damn well please. And finally, there is the fact that there are no restrictions on whom you can have sex with. So many people say that when they become involved in relationships, they are ready to go cold turkey in regard to everybody else – that they are ready to make that lifelong commitment. But far too many times, the truth is that these people act on impulsiveness more than anything else. And proof of this is when the all too often adversity rears its ugly head. When the sex gets boring, people start to think 'I used to fuck other people when the sex would get boring. Now I can't do that because I'm in a relationship.' When a person can't sleep and wants to get up at four in the morning and go take a walk but can't because the significant other won't give him or her the okay, people will start to think 'I used to be able to get up at anytime I wanted to – to take a walk anywhere I wanted to, but now I can't because I'm in a relationship.' You see, often the bottom line is that the craziness many experience in relationships is little more than a response to the feeling of being trapped in that relationship. You see what so many people fail to realize is that when a person is living single, he or she is the sole decision maker in his or her life. Whatever decisions are made will affect him or her and no explanation will ever be necessary. If at any time an individual feels trapped, whether it is a sexual escapade, which is trying to evolve into a relationship or whether an individual just is not happy, that individual can up and leave on their quest to find happiness. This is the exact opposite of what can be done in a relationship. You see, so many people jump into a relationship and are not prepared for this. They think that whomever they involve themselves with will have the same type of long term goal as they themselves have. They think that because everything is agreeable and agreed upon at the beginning of the relationship, it will continue to be so all throughout the relationship. This is of course until they realize that the individual they decided to involve themselves with is not an opposite sex carbon copy of themselves but someone who may be the exact opposite in thoughts, opinions and actions. And when this realization comes into the realization of the other, that is about the same time that the other starts to say, 'I can't talk to you, you never listen to me, you are always against me' and things like that.

Now there are many types of crazy and there are many interpretations of crazy as well. In fact, it is commonly said that there is a fine line between a genius, a crazy person, and someone who is misunderstood. These are all based on the perspective of the one giving the label. There is also a category, which is many times indistinguishable from crazy, and this category is called hurt. People will do things, which are considered crazy to get back at somebody who has wronged them. Lorena Bobbitt was called crazy when she cut off her husband's you know what. In fact, the reason she was acquitted was because she was labeled temporarily insane. Now granted, I think that abuse is wrong and I do not condone it in any form or fashion, but how in the hell can anyone be crazy for a little while? What I do believe is that in addition to being hurt, extremely hurt, she suffered a loss of control. People don't go crazy and then snap out of it like say the protocol behind a nightmare. People do get really, really fucking mad, however – and then eventually get over whatever it was that originally made them mad. You see, crazy people do not start non profits, as she reportedly did in 2008, for battered women and children. Crazy people are crazy for life. You never hear anybody at the job saying 'yea man, last week my crazy was acting up.' In relationships, people aren't crazy. People act crazy. Dealing with someone who has an actual, legitimate mental disorder, as what many in this world will often mistakenly identify as crazy, is not only a lifelong process, but also a severe and sensitive undertaking. People don't deal with crazy in relationships. People deal with those who act crazy because the acting crazy is what keeps the relationship exciting. It is what keeps the fear of reprisal fresh in the mind of the significant other. If someone were legitimately crazy, this individual would not know right from wrong and would, as in the example described above, probably try and cut off a piece of someone's anatomy, and not as revenge for years of abuse or infidelity, but simply because on a nice, bright, sunny day, the voices in her fucking head would have told her to do so. Very few people in their right mind would deal with this type of unexpected behavior. But you see, there is no textbook crazy behavior that people can use to gauge what is crazy and what is normal on a bad day – unless of course you are speaking of the extreme. Someone stabbing somebody 187 times is extreme by anybody's measure and is what would no doubt be classified as crazy. What people do is say most individuals who are sane would not do this, so if you do anything beyond what most sane people do, then automatically you are crazy.

When it comes to certain types of relationships, people will say thinks like 'I'm just gonna fuck him or her and that'll be it.' But they don't realize that some of these individuals walking around are borderline crazy, and all that is needed is one good orgasm to bring out the insanity. Orgasms have been widely known to bring out stalkers. You may think it is laughable but what is going to happen when you walk out your building and see the person you banged on a drunken whim, stalking you because he or she now believes that they are in love? You see, some people are not crazy when they do things like what was stated in the examples above. Some people are responding to what they interpret as hurt. Now even if it is not the intent to hurt the other in the relationship, it is how the other interprets what the first has done or is doing, which will dictate his or her actions. This is why I am asking you, pleading with you, and begging you, please get to know the person you are planning to bang into submission and do it before you start your banging sessions. Some people have been hurt so bad that they will kill you if they are hurt again. And as stated above, the hurt does not have to be intentional. It does not even have to be actual. All it has to be is interpreted as something intentionally done to hurt the other and the other may start on a path of irreversible vengeance.

One reason people continue to overlook when it comes to why relationships fail, even though they do everything they think is right in that relationship or even though they do everything that the significant other wants, is the fact that many out here have real and legitimate issues. Now this is not a stab at the community of individuals suffering from mental health issues, even though many of them do bring quite a bit of drama to relationships. This is about those who do the complete opposite of what is right and expected by the world at large and then expect the world at large to understand and accept. A sad but true fact is that many parents ignore or overlook problems that the young generation has. And this is because they either cannot accurately diagnose these problems or because they do not know what their next course of action is if they can. So they just sweep these problems under the rug and let these problems grow into adulthood. They let these rock chewing children do whatever the fuck it is they want to do and then move these people into an area where acceptance is the norm. I had a conversation recently with someone in regard to the above and about the way society is - and I asked what would happen if one day somebody wanted to fuck a tree? And not only that, what if this individual reasoned that he was actually in love with the tree? And not only that, what if this individual wanted to marry the tree? Would he fall under the 'he's grown and he can do whatever he wants to' realm of understanding? Or would he fall under the one that says he's crazy as shit?' I can hear it now 'I now pronounce you man and tree.' I mean if you think about it, how much different is a tree from a man? If a man fucks a tree, he won't produce any offspring and if that same man fucks another man, guess what? Same result. Yet men are fucking other men and not only that, they are marrying these other men. And society is being forced into accepting. Now here's the crazy thing: people who share this type of thinking sometimes get into relationships with those who don't and you think the relationship they have is going to happily continue when the differences in thought and opinion are so far apart on the spectrum? Highly doubt that. You see, a person's mind has to be understood before a lifelong commitment is established. You CANNOT say 'damn, you look good, I wanna marry you' because your relationship will do one of two things: one; it will fail or two; it will continue, but it will be unhappy as shit.

We always find ways to ignore potential craziness or unhappiness in relationships. And this is because everybody gives off signs. We just don't pay attention to them. This is called the getting to know stage. Countries don't put individuals on watch lists because they feel like doing it. Something has to happen to bring attention. It is the same thing with law enforcement. Something has to happen somewhere in the past to most often make them act the way they do. And it is the same thing with relationships. People have to do something, which gives or will give insight into how they will behave later on down the line, with or without adversity in the relationship. Many times in relationships people will know the person they are interested in has issues or fuck the political correctness, is crazy as shit and they will still become involved with this person. A common example of the crazy some people have is how when a new relationship is initiated and one person may say 'I want you to meet my friends' and the other will respond with 'I don't want to meet anybody you had sex with.' Now this can be a situation of this individual being crazy or at the very least, having certain issues with trust or with feeling threatened. Number one, if you are in this type of relationship, this should be a sign for you to leave. Number two; they feel threatened because they may quite possibly think that the former lover may still have a flame for the one in the new relationship and may be still holding on to the hope that there is always a chance at reconciliation – or at least sex. This type of person will think that sex is paramount and will also think that because you had sex, you will never be able to fully disassociate yourself from the past relationship or the ex won't. And here's the thing: you may be completely cool with your ex lover or ex sex partner without anything sexual going on. But look at how this creates a problem: you could be just hanging out with your ex whom your new significant other may not want to meet or have any type of positive interaction with and your significant other may just happen by. What do you logically think is going to happen? Do you think that this individual is going to say something to the effect of 'hi my name is so & so. I'm Jeremiah's wife. No. That's what you call wishful thinking like a motherfucker because the reality is or more than likely will be something to the effect of 'who the fuck is this bitch?!!' And then when you try to explain to your wonderful and crazy significant other that this other person is just a friend, your wonderful and crazy significant other, after putting you through all types of unnecessary interrogation, will ask that one question, which will more than likely cause your demise or cause detriment like you can only imagine. And that question is did you sleep with this individual?

You see the importance of getting to know the significant other before he or she becomes the significant other is so underrated that people end up getting divorced or separated after basing their lives on avoiding actually getting to know the significant other. Here's an example: Many fast food establishments have to contend with individuals using their rest rooms and not purchasing the products that these restaurants sell. To combat this, these establishments have a policy, which states that a receipt must be shown for entry into the bathroom. They even have security guards enforcing this rule. Now after finding myself caught in a few uncomfortable situations because of this, I began to carry an old receipt around in my pocket. See, I take the proactive role and show the receipt to the guard and I get to use the bathroom without any spills - no problem. I save money and accomplish my goal of relieving myself whenever need be. Now this is not so much about deception as it is preparedness. I am fully aware that if I do not act in this proactive manner, I will have to deal with unfortunate consequences later. And you see, this is the type of preparedness, which needs to be done in relationships. You see, relationships, besides being about expectation and interpretation, are also about preparedness. It is about knowing what the other party is going to do or might possibly do, even before he or she does. It is also about having a plan of attack to deal with whatever occurs, if and when it does. Now I know that no couple in the world will experience every piece of adversity this world has to offer but people should prepare for as many of them as possible. If you have been cheated on in your past relationship or even if you haven't, you should already know that infidelity is a big relationship no-no, so you should already have a plan in place to number one; try your best to prevent it from happening or number two; be quick with a responsive action plan, just in case it does. Unfortunately, what most people do is become involved in a relationship with someone and just make the assumption that the other does not have issues or problems or skipping the political correctness, is fucking crazy because the other has not given any reason to believe that there are issues. There will be those who will prepare for possible adversity when it comes to the significant other but they will only go so far. They will give the other the benefit of the doubt in regard to their sanity. They won't say 'maybe this motherfucker might have a flashback of his days in the military and try to drive us off a bridge.' But you see, this is why people have to do extensive recon into an individual's background before involvement with said individual begins. My advice is don't give the benefit of the doubt to anyone and this is because you never know what an individual will or may do. You never know what triggers you may be unintentionally setting off by doing nothing more than being yourself. When it comes to the preparation for the initiating of a relationship, three background checks must be covered extensively and they are first; criminal, then financial, and last but definitely not least, there is the psychological. You have to make sure that this motherfucker is not cray cray. If you really think about it, the other two are not complete deal breakers. I mean so many people have had infractions of the law and interactions with law enforcement, even in small doses, that to find someone who has had none at all would be as daunting a task as finding a 40 year old virgin.

CHAPTER

8

Needle In A Haystack

There is a well populated belief floating around the intellect of society that there is somebody for everybody. With billions of people presently residing on this planet we call earth, it is incomprehensible to think that there are individuals walking around complaining that they cannot find a significant other. Now exact specifics on how many people exist on this planet are probably never going to be known and this is because people are being born every minute, people are dying every minute and some people live in places so remote, that they may never be found, unless they want to. But to believe that more men were created than women or more women were created than men has to be at the top of my list for complete bullshit. I know that there is also the belief of this ratio thing, which states that there are like six or seven women to every man or some shit like that, but again bullshit, I say. Being that men and women are the only ones who bring forth life of another man or woman, to not have enough equal partners, that would mean that by design, infidelity or

171

promiscuity would be encouraged - or somebody would not have anybody to copulate with and therefore would remain single for all of their days. Does this sound right or fair? Of course not. Everybody needs love, companionship and all that good stuff, so why would there logically be more of one gender than the other? Now what happens after people are born is totally up to them. And by this I mean the decisions they make regarding what gender they want to change into or continue being is what screws up the whole way things were initially planned, and what makes it doubly difficult for people to find a significant other. The problem with finding a significant other, rather the right significant other, is many times hampered by, as stated above people changing into who they want to be instead of who they are supposed to be and having their own criteria list of qualifications.

In regard to finding someone for a relationship

Somebody told me a long time ago that when it comes to finding someone for a relationship, don't go after the person you like, go after the person who likes you. The reason being: that way you will already know that there is interest on the side of the other and you will have at least that on which to build. If you go after somebody you like, you don't know if they like you and you are taking a chance that they will. If they don't like you or are unsure if they do, then you will have to work twice as hard to establish and secure that like. You will have to make them garner interest for one, and second, you will have to work to make them maintain the interest that you have garnered. In addition to this, you will have to find somebody who believes just as you do or as close to the way you do about most of the things in life. Sure opposites attract but you cannot have success in a relationship with someone who agrees with you one minute and with society the next.

In regard to relationships, many people will expect others to be able to jump into a new relationship as soon as the old relationship is finished. They will expect that no time is needed for healing of the mind or emotions. These people feel that if an individual has been involved in a relationship for five, ten or even twenty years, that that individual will be ready to start anew, without any baggage from the past and not have memories of the past relationship interfere with the present relationship. These people are fools. And if you are the type of individual to jump into a new relationship right after leaving a relationship, then sorry but you are not too far from the above description. Some people have this belief of they have to be in a relationship because they cannot stand the idea of being alone. This is understandable but it too, is bullshit. If you cannot stand the thought of being alone, then more than likely you will accept whatever comes and your relationship as well as happiness, will suffer as a result. What people know but don't always focus on long enough to really realize is that whenever there is a traumatic event in their lives, there needs to be a period of healing. When people pass away, very few are capable of saying 'oh well, let's move on.' This is especially true if the departed individual was close. But the expectation is that if you are in a relationship, whether happy or not, once it is over, then so should all recollections, experiences and interactions be as well. This is why relationships experience problems. You cannot love somebody with all of your heart and then extinguish all of that love at the drop of a hat. It just doesn't happen that way. Life is not like that. It may take years to grow to love somebody and to be expected to un love that somebody just because a new relationship has been initiated is nonsense. You see the problem, which too many have is that they go looking for new relationships with those who are seemingly unhappy in their present relationships and then they jump right into a relationship with these people – and even if the relationship is honest and genuine, the fact that the mind has not completely gotten rid of the influence that the previous relationship may hold, will allow for many instances of 'you are not over your last boyfriend, girlfriend, husband or wife' to come in later on in the relationship and piss the new significant other off. This is not one sided either. People in relationships all too often feel that if they leave an unhappy situation by getting involved in a new, seemingly happier situation, that their past situation will automatically be no more and the unhappiness, which was experienced, will be forgotten almost as if it had never happened. Good luck with that. Relationships are not shoes or apparel that, if they outlive their usefulness, are to be discarded, only to be replaced by newer or better items. Relationships involve feelings. And for those of you who may not know, it is probably easier to extricate yourself from a bear trap, than to rid yourself from feelings of a person you love or may once have.

Now I may be alone here but I believe that nothing happens by chance. And by this I mean that the individual you are going to spend your life with is predestined. Somebody has already been chosen for you. You may not know who this person is but I believe that you will find out when the time is right. This thing of searching for Mr. & Mrs. right through dating sites and drunken nights is pointless because the one you are meant to be with will find you or you will find your way to this person - eventually. Look at the way this world is. You do bad and bad will come back to you. You do good and good will find its way to you. And this is because there is cause and effect with everything else in this world but for some reason or other people want to believe that when it comes to relationships, whether it is the meeting of the person you get involved in the relationship with or whether it is what happens within the relationship, everything just happens by chance. Now this is, in my opinion, unequivocal bullshit. Babies don't just happen. You have to do something for their existence to come into being. Accidents don't just happen. If you look at every accident in the world, there is always a logical explanation, leading to either the fault of one or both of the parties involved. Money doesn't appear out of nowhere and neither do wars, which take the lives of thousands or hundreds of thousands. There is <u>always</u> something, which precedes the result. Now while I do believe that somewhere there is someone meant for you and you meant for someone, there has to be some footwork done on the part of the single individual. There needs to be an excessive amount of filtering has to be done when attempting to connect with the one who is meant to be in your life. Now, yes it is possible for you to go out and find the one you were for or who was meant for you but I do believe that the process leading up to this connection will assuredly include some form of trial and error. It is pretty close to an impossible task to meet somebody, get involved, and stay with this individual all of your life, without ever dating or having feelings for anyone else. Don't get me wrong, because the above has happened and probably will continue to do so but it is not that common. Without the excessive filtering, impulsive choices can and will be made, which may prolong the process of meeting the Mr. or Miss Right that you are supposed to meet. So it is very difficult to fathom that a relationship just happens. You have to believe that there is somebody in this world for you. Otherwise you are going to be one of those individuals who do nothing but jump into chain relationships, meaning one right after the other, so that the hurt from the previous relationship does not have a chance to settle into your mind and depress you – or you are going to be one of those individuals who do nothing but jump into bed with random individuals. Either way, you will receive temporary satisfaction. What you and I both know, but may not be willing to admit, is that everybody is looking for lifelong satisfaction.

CHAPTER

9

Sex – It's Not Just For Grown Folks Anymore

When most people think of sex, the first thing they think of is either their last sexual experience, their best sexual experience or the sexual experience that they want to have. In addition to this, the thought process is almost 100% of the time positive. They never think of sex being bad. And why should they? The act of sex is so unbelievably popular because of one significant reason. It feels good! No, it feels great! The problem with this great feeling is that when something feels as good as the act of sex undoubtedly does, there will be chatter about it. People will talk to their friends, co-workers, or families, you name it. They will be as descriptive as possible – sometimes unnecessarily so. The bad thing about all of this talk is that the one group of individuals who should not be hearing about it is the one group who does hear about it and far too often tries to emulate the behavior. That group is the children. Sex is one of the most misunderstood and complex things known to man. It is something, which like many other things in life follows a specific protocol. People get married, and then they have sex. People say they love one another, and then they have sex. People become boyfriend and girlfriend, and then they have sex. This is how things go. But the problem is that sex, instead of being a love building exercise or perhaps a vehicle to have children, is being used as basically something to do. And because it is just done, it will more than likely be just done with no concern of the other parties' enjoyment or satisfaction. You see, this is what is happening with kids all across the country. Children go off by themselves, away from the prying eyes of parents and caretakers to do the unimaginable. They sneak off into staircases, backyards, unlocked school playgrounds and the like and experiment with being grown ups. They indulge in the sex act without protection, without concern for ramifications and without instruction other than you stick it in or you let him stick it in and then you move back and forth - then people wonder why certain ramifications occur. Now pregnancy and disease are two of the major negative consequences, which can occur from learning about physical intimacy in this manner. But there are others and aside from the misconstrued feelings of attachment, there is a major negative which comes in the form of thinking that that type of sex is the only way sex is and the only way sex will ever be. You see when young people are banging out a quickie in the back of somebody's building or in a public park (and believe it or not, this happens more than you may think) they are not caressing each other. They are not whispering terms of endearment. They are not trying to make the sex act the best that the other has ever had. What they are most likely doing is attempting to finish before they get discovered. They are trying to have a story to tell. You see young people have to sneak around when they want to show their affections for their chosen love interest and this is because nine times out of ten, they are too young to have an adult type of relationship where sex is welcomed anyway. So while they are doing this 'get it wherever you can' type of intercourse, they are cementing the thought that each time I have sex, it's going to be like this. And when these people grow up and get into relationships, if this behavior is not challenged, then it will carry over into adult relationships, were the significant other will most assuredly be unsatisfied. The thing about this is that you cannot blame the people in relationships because they are only reliving what they have been taught or what they have taught themselves as children. The parents aren't really to blame because nine times out of ten, there was no instruction regarding sex other than 'don't you bring your ass in here pregnant' or 'don't you go and get anybody out here pregnant.' But then again the parents do have to shoulder some of the responsibility because had they had a tighter leash on some of these kids, they would not be out here connecting with every swinging dick or loose vagina, which allows them to do so. Society and the educational system must be held accountable too. You see by the time they teach sex education in many of the schools, many of the kids have already put the lesson into practice several times over. It is more than a crying shame that kids are experimenting with sexual activity at the ages of ten and eleven but parents and the powers that be are waiting to teach kids about the proper way to either abstain or have sex when they become high school students. You see what many people do not realize is that children are tape recorders. They watch these adult only programs on television and with no inkling of an idea of what they are doing, they go and try to do what they see being done on television, in real life. Society feels that when you get involved in a relationship, you are already supposed to know everything to do in that relationship but the parents won't teach the kids and the schools will teach them only so much and usually when it's about close to too late, what else are these young people to do? Simple, they start watching porn. They start watching porn first for the wonder and then for the education. Now understand, this is not the totally unheard of thing when it comes sex. Some people's only teaching of lovemaking is the porno. Many of those people watch porn for years upon years and some even grow up on the indulgence of it.

These people then get into relationships and try and relive the teachings from the porn tutelage. They try to bang the shit out of the significant other. They try to have sex with many partners and they try to have their partner have sex with many partners and try to do any and every position known to man. Basically they try and do everything, which they learn from the sex movies. Now the blame for this unfortunately has nowhere to land because even though a man can teach a boy how to be a man, can you imagine dear old dad saying 'son, this is how you fuck.' And even fewer sons are going to ask their dads or father figures for instruction. This is where friends come in. Friends will have no problem saying 'I had this bitch doing this and doing that. I had her legs up here and I was going forty miles per hour and so on and so forth.' However parents, no matter how open minded and free spirited they may be, might find explaining things in a graphic manner such as that, a tad bit objectionable - especially a father talking to a daughter. I mean can you fucking imagine? 'Honey, your boyfriend is going to take you like this and bend you like that and so on and so forth...' It just doesn't happen. And this is why couples have issues in the bedroom. You see, kids, yes kids, have been fucking in staircases, in school bathrooms and in public parks for the longest of time. These kids are not taught the proper techniques or the proper amount of love, which is required to even indulge in the act before they do the act. All they are taught is part A goes into part B and it's supposed to feel good. What happens then? These kids grow up with the same methodology and mindset and when they get into relationships, it is almost a certainty that one of the two will be unsatisfied.

Now undoubtedly, the act of sex is one of life's most joyous pleasures. It is the only two-fold entity, which gives guaranteed pleasure on both ends. You have sex, you get a baby. You don't get a baby, it still feels good practicing. (Most times anyway) Many years ago, the act of sex was for the sole purpose, okay maybe not sole purpose but main purpose was to procure a child. People would get married and then have sex. They would raise the child in the traditional way with integrity and values and such, so that when the child, who was conceived through wedlock, reached adulthood, he or she would do the same thing. Somewhere along the line, that shit got flipped like a motherfucker. Now people are fucking for every reason under the sun, except for that of having children. And that's not the entirety of the bad part either. The ones who are doing all of this wanton fucking without regard for ramifications are getting younger and younger and younger. Now it is no secret that untrained and unknowledgeable people are having and raising kids everyday. The problem is that the powers that be for some reason or other cannot seem to make the connection between the overwhelming lack of education and the seemingly unavoidable breakdown of society. You see since there is no restriction of who can stick a dick into whom, stupid people can have kids, retarded people can have kids, even those with serious developmental issues can produce a child. The problem is that with all of these groups and more screwing whenever they get the chance, the world will become populated with more stupidity, more retardation and more of those with those with severe mental issues. You see, teachers allow children to fail in school by giving them passing grades when they have not earned them, so that the overall perception of the institution will be positive. Parents allow children to fail at home by sitting them in front of the television day in and day out. And the kids only allow themselves a break when its time to eat or when they have to go to the bathroom. People allow children to fail in society by eventually giving them dead end jobs, which will never allow them to live better than a minimum wage existence. And then what happens is these people who have these educational and sometimes mental issues, learn little more than how to dress really nicely, depend on the assistance of others, and meet up with you. Then these people who know nothing more than how to wiggle a dick or bounce up and down on one are causing more detriment in the relationship than what is humanly feasible. You see too many people have this belief that relationships are about and will sustain themselves because of love. This is bullshit. Relationships are about education and attraction. The young people indulging in sexual activity usually only focus on one and here's a hint: it's not education. They see something, which looks good and they either want to stick it or get stuck by it. Then they want to learn about the person after the fact. This is more bullshit. Too many young people and those with the young person's mindset have no plan for the future. They proactively think with the reactive mind. In other words, let's fuck now and take the relationship day by day. When money issues come, we will deal with them then. If a child is conceived through our fuck sessions, whether by accident or by one of us planning, we will again deal with it when the situation occurs. So many people in this world know that this is not the best option for success, yet they still try. And this is why couples have unnecessary problems.

When some people are young, they are taught have a plan for the future. Some of those young people interpret this as have a varied portfolio of stocks. Other young people interpret this as having at least one consistently growing bank account. And still others make the interpretation having a stable of significant others. When it comes to the stable of significant others, these young people will have sex with somebody with no intention of returning after the sex act or with no intention of a relationship. All they will want is to give the other the best sex he or she has ever indulged in and the reason why is because months or years down the line, the only recollection, which will be had is the memory of good, rather great sex and no unhappiness to go along with it – the opposite of what happens in relationships. You see in relationships, patterns of unhappiness are what cause people to break up. Years later, if people break up, they may remember the sex but it will be attached to the bad memories of the break up or the unhappy relationship. Many people cannot separate sex from emotions. In other words, they will mistake good sex for love. And this is what many people bank on. They will think that since the only memories they have are of good sex and no unhappy relationship, then this individual will always be able to provide that good sex and happiness which comes along with it. When it comes to relationships, many of them are initiated because of the investment protocol. And by this I mean people will invest so much, whether that investment is financial, emotional support or just the general being there for whatever situation arises, which cannot be handled alone, that the other will have no choice but to pay them back. The roi or return on this investment is a type of guilt, which leads to the obligation to pay back the initial investment by the other party. And the way the investment is almost always paid back is through a relationship, whether it is sexual or an actual long term type of thing.

CHAPTER

~~10~~

Honesty In Relationships

There is one thing, which I believe is searched for more than all searches on the World Wide Web and that is total honesty in relationships. The reason why I believe it is searched for so extensively is because it simply does not exist. As a rule, people desire honesty in relationships. They expect it. They crave it. They want whomever they decide to drop their defenses and pants to, to be as honest are they are to them. Now this, by all estimation, is a not an unreasonable expectation. I mean if I don't cheat on you and I don't lie to you, I would hope that at the very least, you would respect me enough to reciprocate. Unfortunately life is not always how we would like or expect. Sometimes there are bad people in this world who do bad things and who ironically continue to get involved with good people on the complete opposite side of the spectrum. Now the idea of complete honesty is as with everything else in this world, up to interpretation. Complete honesty to me could mean I will tell you everything. Period. And I will not hold back, sugarcoat or omit anything to make the complete honesty easier for you to handle. On the opposite end of the spectrum, complete honesty to somebody else could mean I will be as honest as I can to you as long as it does not cause you any type of unhappiness. Now I am sure that we will all agree, this is not complete honesty. But what too many people in relationships do is use this type of interpretation of honesty to ensure that their relationships continue unbothered. What people do not realize is that relationships are full of hypocrisy. If you tell the complete truth in relationships, which is much desired, many will become upset because they are incapable of handling the complete truth in any form or fashion. If you do not tell the complete truth, the significant other may label you a liar, and not only that, may continue to believe and treat you as such, even if the lies which were told, were told for the benefit of the relationship. Crazy right? Relationships are full of nonsense and one of the biggest pieces of nonsense in relationships is the 'I don't care how bad it hurts, please tell me the truth.' This is so common. People ask for this because they, for some reason or other feel that whatever truth they are about to receive is not going to be that bad. They have this perpetual belief that in the long run, the truth will make for a better relationship. Maybe the above would be true if this were a perfect world and people were perfect in their thinking and understanding.

But this world is not perfect and so many people have issues in their thinking and understanding of things that telling the truth to certain individuals will cause nothing but detriment to the truth telling individual. Now some people may argue that it is not the truth but how you relay it, which is the dangerous thing and to an extent I agree but there are many situations where tact is completely ineffective – and dealing with a crazy individual is one of those situations. One of those other situations, which has nothing to do with crazy, is the one of an individual not understanding, never being able to understand what the significant other is attempting to relay to him or her or not willing to accept what the significant other is attempting to relay. And a prime example of this is how many men will tell a woman that they are not looking for a relationship, just a sexual encounter. This can occur before a relationship, sexual or otherwise, is had or it can occur soon thereafter. Many women who are in search of the truth from the man they are involved in or interested in will fathom that the man is just a dog, can't handle a real relationship or wants a real relationship but has not yet reached that level of maturity where he realizes that deep down that is exactly what he wants. But one thing that many of these women fail to realize is that for many men, that right there is possibly the truest truth you will ever receive. You see what often happens in people's lives is they get so happy and elated at the prospect of a relationship and at the prospect of someone whom they like, actually liking them, that many times they will hear what this person says but they will not completely listen. So when an individual says they do not want a relationship, the other person will interpret that as they don't want a relationship right now. While one says I am not looking for a relationship right now but means I am not looking for a relationship ever, the other will think that this person means he doesn't yet know what he wants and will eventually come around to the thinking of the other when he finds out that the other is everything a good woman or wife should be.

CHAPTER

11

Infidelity Is Something We All Face In One Form Or Another

One of the biggest questions in the world of existence, is the one of why do people cheat? And the answer to that question is that's a good damned question. You see there is no one answer as to why people cheat. People cheat for many different reasons, and sometimes people cheat for one specific reason. The thing which people have an inexplicably hard time understanding, is that you will never be able to answer a general question such as that without a specific targeted individual. The question people need to ask is why does or why would the man or woman I am involved with think it's okay to cheat? Now the number of reasons surrounding why some individuals decide to cheat are astronomical. Some people give the reason for their being unfaithful as no sex being had or not enough sex being had in their relationship. Some give the reason for infidelity as the sex not being enjoyable, and some will even give a reason as incredulous as 'I don't know why, I just did it.' Now the act of infidelity itself is never so much a problem as what happens before and after said act occurs. People do not realize that there will always be things, which push an individual toward infidelity (and many of those are done unwittingly by the significant other) and there are things, which allow the infidelity to continue, which are many times based on the reactions of the first act of infidelity.

Infidelity has probably been around since the beginning of time. The thing about infidelity is that it and a relationship are almost the exact same because they are both up to the interpretation of the individuals involved. There are many who will immediately discard this bit of information because they will feel that everybody's interpretation of infidelity is the same but here's the thing: <u>some people do not feel having more than one relationship is cheating if they do not consider themselves in a relationship to begin with.</u> This is probably the most basic lesson of understanding the basics of a relationship. Some people feel that if sex is had, then a relationship is underway or a relationship is sure to follow. Other people feel that if sex is had, then that is the extent of their involvement in the other individual's life, unless of course there is the need or desire for more sex. These are two completely different and acceptable interpretations of types of relationships. These are both okay. The problem comes in when these two types of people get together. And this happens *ALL THE*

TIME. Now here's the thing: most people will more than likely say, I can tell when my significant other is cheating or I know that my significant other's interpretation of what I want our relationship to be is the same as what I want it to be. This is the problem. You never know what is on the mind of another person, no matter what they tell you. And this is because people lie. People lie. People fucking lie. They lie to protect feelings. They lie because they fear ramifications. They lie because they don't know how to tell the truth. The reason so many relationships end is because people live according to what they believe instead of what they know for certain. And the even bigger problem is that people in relationships almost never tell the significant other the complete truth about what they want in regard to the relationship if it is not what the significant other wants. Now what you have is basically two types of deception. The first is between each party in the relationship about the status or depth of the relationship and then you have the guilty party in the relationship being deceptive about the cheating, which has occurred. You see people all the time use as a defense the 'I didn't cheat on you because we are not in a relationship.' Okay but here's the thing: sex creates relationships. And these relationships do not always have to include a child (although many times they do). The type of relationship that a sexual encounter creates is one comprised mainly of feelings. And the problem with this is that when you are in a relationship, a happy and progressive relationship, there is no room to do anything but share your feelings with the significant other and family. Think about this for a second; a man can be married, have a child or two and a mistress. Do you think it will be possible for him to just have feelings for the wife and family and not the mistress? Here's an even better question: do you think it will be possible for the mistress to not have feelings for the man? It may be possible, but I for one have never seen it happen and I have experienced many adulterous relationships – experienced, not indulged in. You see the thing about feelings is that they will always be prevalent, even if they are suppressed to the point of non existence. When feelings are shared between family and an 'outside influence' as what cheating is often called, there will be a period of the one sharing those feelings becoming distant. And overlooking a significant other becoming distant is many times one of the things, which allows infidelity to manifest and continue. You see, it's sad to say but sometimes in relationships you have to be on top of your partner as if he or she were a child. And the reason why is because to quote an old adage, idle hands are the devil's playthings. If some people are left to their own devices, they will many times allow themselves to be led astray. You see, everybody is not as educated as they appear to be, as morally

196

grounded as they portray or as able to resist temptation as you yourself may be. And this is why many times you have to show up at the job unannounced, call them at weird hours when they are not with you, just to make sure they answer their phone, and once in a blue moon, answer their phone so that whomever may be even remotely thinking about impeding on your territory, will be made aware of not only your presence but also the fact that your ass is crazy enough to jab their fucking eyes out if they even think about messing up your happy home.

Now when it comes to why people cheat, as stated above, there are so many reasons for its occurrence. Some of those reasons are well known and some, not well known at all. Some of them are verified, legitimate excuses, and some are straight up bullshit. One of those reasons, which teeter totters between not well known and legitimate, is a thing known as sexual addiction. The big problem about sexual addiction is that people who suffer from it either don't know they do or don't find out until after the relationship is well underway. Either way, they are not going to tell you. Many guys for instance, don't believe that they can be addicted to sex. And this is because a lot of men are taught to get all the sex they can, from as many as they can, so more than likely they will think that having random and continuous sexual escapades is just a normal part of their existence. In addition, there is no chart, which says if you have sex with this many partners, as opposed to that many or you do these types of activities in your relationship, then you are addicted. And this is because while in many relationships, couples try and do everything sexually they can think of anyway. The problem is when the wanton sexual acts, which are supposed to be only shared between a committed couple starts to seep into the outside world. The time when the 'addiction' becomes a problem is when it starts to hurt, when it starts to cause detriment in the relationship, when an individual puts the sexual gratification above family and employment, and even when this individual goes outside of the relationship to find that satisfaction.

Now in regard to cheating: some people will have you believing that all men cheat at some point or other in their lives. This is not true. I am severely inclined to believe that all men are tempted, as are all women but it is not the fact that everyone is tempted as much as it is the fact of how everyone responds to that temptation. This is why you must understand the person behind the penis and the vagina. Understanding their mind, understanding what they personally have been trained to do and understanding what it is they are more likely to do because of their environment and upbringing, will many times dispel the belief that everybody is a cheat at sometime in their lives. This is why you must, for a happy relationship, think for two people. The first is you. The second is your significant other. Too many people want to take the advice of their friends as law, especially when they think that it will do nothing but help their relationship. But here's the thing about that: many of the people who love to give advice on what to do in infidelity based situations, have been hurt in infidelity based situations or know of people who have. And the advice they give comes directly from that hurt so it more than likely will be negative. You have to wonder, what type of reconciliation can anybody possible expect to hope for when all you are bombarded with is 'that motherfucker is no good' or 'that bitch ain't shit?' You see the hurt from infidelity is one of the harshest that an individual can experience. That, combined with the history of infidelity extending to if your significant other cheats on you, there must be something wrong with you to make him or her cheat and there must especially be something wrong with him or her to want to cheat in the first place, will make it 10x times as hard to forgive and attempt to get the relationship back on track.

Life has many expectations. Some are normal and some are down right retarded. Some will be about how you should live your life and some will be about how you live in your relationship. When it comes to your relationship and the thought of infidelity, people will expect you to be able to multitask in every aspect of your life . except when it comes to your interpretation of relationships. In other words, you can wash dishes and help your children with homework – or you can record a podcast while working on a term paper. You can even drive while doing your make up but you can only love one person at a time. You cannot, according to society, love one person and just fuck another because society says you have to love everybody you fuck. Now we all know or should know that this expectation is bullshit but this is how people think. This is the crazy hypocrisy that makes relationships and those who decide to involve themselves in them go completely off the deep end sometimes. Society will allow anybody to multitask. In fact it is often encouraged, especially in a workplace situation. But people for some strange reason or other seem to frown on the idea of individuals' multitasking when it comes to relationships. They feel that relationships are the only thing in this world, which are immune from doubling up on. They feel that you cannot love one person and have sex with another and still love the first. I mean don't get me wrong but isn't the basic idea behind multitasking? Now many people will say that's bullshit. Once you love somebody, that love is supposed to stay encompassed around the individual you are in love with for the rest of your days. I must say I am inclined to agree but here's the thing: not everybody in this world thinks in this manner nor will they agree. They will more than likely feel that it is okay to multitask, just as long as you do not let feelings become a part of the scenario. Now one of the main reasons that infidelity is often so difficult to understand is because of the your interpretation is different than my interpretation thing. For instance one person may screw somebody based on the fact that he or she seems appealing enough to screw and nothing more but the significant other may deem that one action as only being done because there is love or actual feelings of commitment and attachment. What must be remembered is that many people do things on a whim. This is fact. They take advantage of opportunities as well. This is also fact. Most people do not focus so much on the fact that things were done as much as they focus on why. And when it comes to infidelity, there almost never is enough why to explain why someone has committed it. Now there is something, which is closely related to the not understanding of infidelity and this is the stupid ass philosophy that many law enforcement officials abide by. It is what is called ignorance of the law is no excuse. This means that you are liable for breaking laws that you may not even know are laws. Now anybody with any common sense at all can surely see that this is bullshit in its purest form. I mean who in this world knows every law, which is on the books? Even fucking law enforcement does not know all of the laws, which are in place in every state, city country or province, so how in the world do they expect the random individual to know? I guess they figure that because of your ignorance, sooner or later you are gonna fuck up so we might as well capitalize on your wrongdoing. The thing, which is easily relatable or comparable to relationships, is that because an individual doesn't know what is 'law' to the other person, the other person has the right to basically flip out at any time and for any reason they feel their laws have been violated. But again, what does this go back to? The getting to know part of the relationship. You see just like not everybody in this world will learn all of the laws of the land in which they live, not everybody in relationships will learn all there is to know about what will piss the significant other off in regard to the relationship. Unfortunately what people do is think and say 'you should know you are not supposed to cheat' 'you should know what a woman is in need of' 'you should know what you are supposed to do for a man' and so on and so forth. You see if there was one rule to sum up the cause of all relationship problems in the world especially infidelity, it would be this: learn all you can about a situation before you involve yourself in the situation. Learn all you can about law so that law enforcement officials cannot mistakenly use the law against you. Learn all you can about an individual before you involve yourself with this individual. The keyword here is learn.

The way people act before they get involved in a relationship is often a very good indicator of how they will act once they are in a relationship. So many people know this tidbit of information that it astounds me to the utmost that people seem surprised when the before individual shows up later on in the relationship to take the place of the after the relationship has been initiated individual. You see the thing about people and their infinite relationship wisdom is that they think that whatever they see at the beginning of the relationship is everything they need to see and everything they will continue to see all throughout the relationship. They completely ignore the fact of what the individual may have shown them before, even if it is completely different than what is shown when the relationship is begun. And see this is what people need to pay attention to. The belief that an individual can change from player to priest or whore to housewife, in an instant and have that change last for the rest of his or her natural life is about as believable as a law enforcement official being completely honest. I am not saying it cannot happen; it is just a highly improbable probability. When many people get married or undertake the venture of trying to exist in a committed way of living for years upon years, and without a certain number of years of practice, it is the equivalent of going cold turkey. In other words, a good majority of them will fail. Too many people will get years and years of practice of doing the wrong thing and then when they find somebody whom they feel would make an adequate partner in a relationship, they try and convince themselves, as well as the man or woman in the relationship that they will be faithful – and this my friends is bullshit. I mean don't get me wrong, the attempt at being on the straight and narrow for the rest of the individual's life is about the most noble thing somebody could probably do but that is the expectation. The expectation is nowhere near the actuality. The actuality states that most people who attempt to stop doing what they have been doing for the majority of their lives, will not only fail <u>but will fail miserably.</u> Now look at this from the perspective of commitment. When people get married, they expect that the other, no matter what has been done up until the point of commitment will have no bearing or influence on the future relationship. They expect the person to be good. They expect the person to be perfect. They do not want to hear anything about 'hey baby, you know how I was. You can't just snatch that life away from me. I need to be weaned off of the availability of any time, anyplace ass the same way a baby is weaned off a bottle.' I know it may sound funny but this is how many people think.

Can The Act Be Prevented?

With all of the above stated reasons why an individual may find the need to cheat, another individual may be asking himself well what can I do to guarantee that somebody will not cheat on me? The answer is nothing. Absolutely nothing. Depressing thought, isn't it? Although the reasons, which drive an individual in a relationship to cheat, are most often shared either equally or not, by both parties, the actual act of cheating is a lone decision, which is made by the cheater himself or herself. People are far too often under the mistaken impression that if they do everything, which is considered 'right' in the relationship, that infidelity will never be a factor in their relationship. This thought process is one of the main reasons why infidelity so easily infects many so called happy relationships. People feel that there is this expectation of equality, which hovers over both parties in the relationship once the relationship is initiated. What this expectation of equality states is that whatever one says and believes, the other will accept and believe as well. The other will live according to how the other expects them to as well. And this is supposed to occur whether or not the other individual is aware of the expectation, which is placed above his or her head. All an individual can really do regarding the prevention of the occurrence of infidelity is talk. This means talk about everything, which goes on in the relationship.

Talk about everything from the beginning of the relationship all the way up to the present point in the relationship. People need to talk about what happened in the last relationship regarding infidelity. Talk about what led up to the act of infidelity occurring. Talk about the sex act and what is missing from the sex act, which could make it not only better, but the best it could be. Talk about what would happen if someone were to approach the significant other with an offer of infidelity. And the way to maximize those talks is to have the conversations way before the relationship is long underway. You see the problem that too many people have in relationships is that they make the relationship all about sex, ignore conversation topics as stated above, then when infidelity becomes apart of their relationship, they want to focus on why. Classic reactive vs. proactive way of thinking. The only true thing that an individual can do to ensure a significant other is not cheating on him or her is to follow this individual's activities daily and nightly. Monitor this individual's phone calls and computer communications. In short, be this individual's shadow. My question is: does anybody in this world want to be in a relationship with someone who has to do this? I know I don't. Too many people have this belief that if the significant other is not checking an occasional email or handing out the once in a while who's that when the other is on the phone, that there is no concern in the relationship. My question is this: why would you need to worry that much anyway unless there is no trust in the relationship to begin with? Now of course there is a definite difference between general interest, concern and suspicion but if you knew the person you were involved in a relationship with, and you knew what he or she had the propensity to do regarding the continuance of the relationship, would it really be necessary to monitor this individual's activities as if they were children? I think not. I mean think about how this sounds: 'I have to check up on my man or woman every now and then to make sure that he or she does not stray or feel the need to be tempted.' This is what parents do to children. Ask yourself, are you dating a child? If so, then there is something wrong with you, not the one you are involved in the relationship with. Trust is one of the most difficult things in the world to learn. It is twice as difficult to re learn after it has been destroyed. This is why when relationships are initiated on sex and little else, they will fail or they will not be happy – unless the relationship is only about sex. When relationships are brought about while one or both parties are in unhappy relationships, there will always be the thought that since you cheated with me while you were in a relationship, what guarantee do I have that you won't cheat on me with somebody else when our relationship is unhappy?

Using Innocent Messages To Break Down Defenses

There are certain things, which should not be done in relationships. These things fall under the category of know better. In other words you should just damned well know better. The problem that too many people in this world have is that they don't know better. Nobody has taught them these things that even the most ignorant imbecile should know. Now one of those things that the most ignorant imbecile should know is the very basic rule of not hurting the one you are in a relationship with. The thing which makes this rule such a problem is the fact that people do not know what hurts or is likely to hurt the significant other. One of those hurtful things is when an individual who is not in a relationship sends or relays to someone in a relationship a message or idea, which is sexual or explicit in nature. The main reason this is done is to see if the person in the relationship will respond. And if there is a response, the response will be seen as an invitation to further advances. Now what the people who are targeted will more than likely say is that it was nothing, it was innocent and a whole host of other things to calm the significant other's concerns but here's the thing: sometimes the concerns had by the significant other are valid. And the one downplaying those concerns as unreasonable fears could unwittingly be playing right into the hands of the one attempting to intercede his or her way into the relationship. Social media is the main culprit of this nowadays. It used to be something as small as a dirty joke, which would initiate the conversation about sex. Then, once the conversation about sex has been started, the initiator would continue to pursue topics of a sexual nature. And the more topics the person in a relationship would entertain, the closer the other would feel he or she is to an actual sexual relationship. Now, it doesn't even have to be a dirty joke. Social media has made it so easy to bring up the topic of sex that damn near everybody is participating in these online surveys about favorite sexual positions and which type of sex is the best. And it is all done under the guise of innocent, playful banter, which doesn't mean anything. But here's the thing: it does mean something. People will forward these messages to you and wait for you to respond and once you do, they will fathom that there must be some unhappiness or adversity in your relationship. They will further fathom that if there were no unhappiness or adversity in your relationship, why would you even respond to the message? You see, this is why some people in relationships have to be cruel and heartless to others. They have to be like 'no motherfucker, I don't have time for you! Yes, my entire existence is only comprised of my husband or wife and family!' This is because some people are taught never take no for an answer. Some people are taught that if there is ever any sign of less than complete happiness or any type of hesitation when asked about the status of a relationship, then that sign should be taken as an invitation to offer ones' services at trying to make the relationship better. And most people feel that the only services they can offer is the one of their penis or their vagina. This is why if you are in a relationship and you do not want the added attention, then simply do not allow for it to enter your personal space. If you are on one of these social media sites and your 'friend' sends a group message asking your favorite sexual position, place or anything even remotely related to sex, the only answer you should be sending back is the one of 'I don't indulge in things of that nature.' And the reason why is because you never know who is monitoring your response. You could say 'I love it like this, 15x a day, with several different partners' and your friend may say 'girl, you so crazy' but someone else on that social media site whom you had no intention on seeing your response may have done just that, and not only that, this individual may use that to classify you, fantasize about you and possibly stalk you for the rest of your days.

Being Alone In The Midst Of A Relationship

The not always realized fact is that there is no honor when it comes to infidelity. People will cheat with anybody, anytime, anywhere. Your girlfriend will sleep with your man. Your bff whom you have known for years, will sleep with your man. Nothing in this world trumps the heart and the related feelings, which go along with it. People who seem to have the highest morality will often sacrifice that morality based on the number or type of enticements. A woman will cheat with a man just because he is better in the bedroom than the one she is in a relationship with. A man will cheat with a woman just because he believes that it is in his nature to do so. These, and about a gazillion other reasons are why the act of infidelity is perpetrated. But quite often, society at large will try and compartmentalize the reasons down to only a handful. They will say men cheat because they are dogs. Women cheat because their emotional needs are not being met. They will make it seem like the one who committed the indiscretion is the only one at fault for the indiscretion. Things like this type of thinking and guidance are what destroys and will continue to destroy relationships for evermore. There are two things that everybody inside and outside of a relationship should know. The first is that whenever a relationship goes well, two people are responsible. This means when people stay happily married, raise successful and productive children to adulthood, etc.

two people are responsible. On the opposite side of the spectrum, when a relationship goes bad, as what happens with infidelity, two people are also responsible. For some reason or other there is this worldwide perception, which states that the individual who committed the physical act is the only one guilty of doing something detrimental to the relationship. This is not always the case. Many times, the innocent party may turn a blind eye to what is occurring in his or her relationship before the actual cheating act occurs. There may be weeks, months or years of becoming distant, which the significant other either ignores or does not realize. There may be those unspoken cries for attention, affection or intimacy, which go unnoticed. And a major way this happens is by one party in the relationship working all the time, thereby leaving little to no time to care for the significant other or his or her needs. It does not even have to be a situation of employment. Many times in relationships, people get so caught up in their own lives that they totally and unintentionally ignore the significant other. They stay on the phone all day long. They stay on social media all day long. They take care of the kids and everybody else, all day long, while leaving little to no time for the significant other. This is how people in relationships can feel alone. What helps this feeling is the gender separation. Many women will feel that because men are men, they are always tough and unfeeling and they don't need to be held or talked to the way women do. These women will feel that men don't need to just talk because the men will feel like the women are nagging. But they are so wrong. It is not what you do as much as it is how you do it. When those in relationships feel like the significant other is not there for them, they will go in search for companionship elsewhere. But here's the thing: they will usually never tell the other that they are in need of more attention for fear of them being classified as needy or clingy. Yet when infidelity becomes a part of the relationship, the one who never provided the extra attention will be the first to say that he or she did everything in the relationship that he or she was supposed to do or asked to do and will therefore reason that the other's decision to cheat was solely the decision and fault of the other.

The Why Of Infidelity

When it comes to infidelity, there are three major questions that an individual who has been on the receiving end of it is likely to ask. The first is why. The second is why and the third is why motherfucker? I was good to you. Why would you do this to me? You see, that question right there, that logic of expectancy, is why many relationships fail due to infidelity. People get involved on this whole 50/50 belief system thing, which is coupled with a great deal of expectancy. They are under the impression that whatever is done in a relationship by one party is automatically reciprocated by the other. This is wrong. This has always been wrong. People are going to do whatever they want to do in this world and rarely do they even give half a fuck about how whatever they are doing is going to affect another individual. The only time that there is any type of concern for another individual is when they have a vested interest in that individual, like say for instance, that individual is someone they are in a relationship with – but even then, the concern is on a case by case basis. People always ask if a person has a good man or woman in their lives why would they feel the need to cheat? This question shows the level of ignorance in the world of relationships. Nobody knows everything, which goes on in a relationship. Nobody in a relationship will ever tell everything, which is not going right either. People are too much under the impression that because an individual looks good or gorgeous, that there is no reason to cheat but is this to say that only ugly men have performance problems? Is this to say only unattractive women do not drive a man crazy? Of course not. This is why you will have a good looking man cheating with an unattractive woman and vice versa. It is almost never just about looks and it is almost never just about sex. I mean don't get me wrong, sometimes an individual with cheat with someone just because this individual is the most attractive he or she has seen in his or her life. But this does not mean that there is anything else connected with the act. What people need to realize is that there is pretty girl sex and there is ugly girl sex. There are some things that some pretty women just won't do. The belief is that pretty girls won't ever do what the ugly girls will. The pretty girls for example, historically will not take a money shot to the face but the not so pretty girls, no problem. This is one of the reasons why there are massive problems in relationships. Many guys who grow up watching porn and related trash get to see pretty and beautiful women doing the most vile and disgusting things imaginable. This does nothing but make many of them carry along the belief that all the pretty and beautiful girls are going to do the same thing – or that everybody has a price for their self respect. See, a lot of men want ugly girl perks and behavior from a pretty girl but many of these pretty girls only indulge in pretty girl behavior. So when the random man comes at the random pretty girl with 'hey honey, lick my ass.' Honey is more than likely going to look at random guy like 'are you out of your fucking mind?!!'

On the opposite end of the spectrum, there are some not so pretty women who will do any and everything for acceptance, money or both. The twisted belief of society will lead the average individual to believe that if a man has a pretty woman then he will never deal with a woman not so pretty and this is because much of society thinks that when you have sex with somebody, you love them. Wrong. This always has been wrong. Elsewhere in this publication, I spoke of a reason for cheating being that of unrealized fantasies. If an individual wanted to do something that the person he or she is in a committed relationship with would never do, is it fair to assume that the lusting or longing for that desire will go away just because the other will not ever do it? Of course not. Again - relationships are about the expectation that whatever I want is whatever you want and if I don't want it or think that you should not have it, then guess what? You're not gonna have it. Now going back to the pretty girl, ugly girl thing, it is possible that an individual may have the most raunchy, disgusting, pee on me and I will do the same to you type of intimacy, only because this is something that is no more than a fantasy instilled in the mind of this individual by porn or the overactive imagination of friends. But it does not mean that there is any type of love for the individual who was recruited for this instance nor does it mean there is any love lost for the individual in the relationship who hopefully does not know about this occurrence. By the way, this is not limited to gender. Men and women both have demented fantasies. The bottom line is this; when you prevent somebody from doing something that he or she has always wanted to do, you cannot reasonably expect that they will automatically stop wanting to do it. Is it right? No. Is it normal? That's the question you need to examine.

The reasons for why an individual would commit the act of infidelity are so varied and sometimes unexplainable, that it may be impossible to ever accurately detail them all. However there are some major ones, which always seem to show up whenever the act is perpetrated. Some people do not realize that when it comes to reasons for infidelity, the you are not what I want, you are what I accept, ranks way up in the top percentage. Sure, everybody wants to say that there is something wrong with the man because he cheated or that there is something with the woman because he cheated on her but few ever stop to think that the relationship is fraudulent from the beginning. It is many times a situation of 'you have my attention, but not my heart.' You see people turn a blind eye to deception clues in the beginning of relationships all the time. People show signs of craziness before the relationship is initiated and people still get involved. People show signs of violence before the relationship is initiated and people still get involved. People show signs of future infidelity and people still get involved. Many people will inquire well why would somebody get involved with me if he or she really does not like me? And this question right there shows how much the presence of deception is ignored in many people's lives and relationships. People can be turned off by someone they had interest in within a nanosecond. It can be because of the person's attitude. It can be because of the person's political beliefs. It can be because of a person's breath. It can even be due to a person's hatred of another race or religion. But here's the thing: people will have sex with those they hate every other thing about, all the time. These people will determine that for whatever reason the one that once held their interest is no longer relationship material but is still prime sexual material and because of that fact sex will be had but the relationship will be purely in the mind of the other. People won't say listen, I thought I liked you but I changed my mind. No they will continue with the façade for as long as they are able. You see people can fake a relationship for years. 'I don't like you but I like fucking you.' Sound familiar? The problem is that too many in this world are desperate for companionship. Instead of putting an individual through the wringer so to speak to make sure that he or she is long term relationship material, many people will ask a few questions, have a few drinks and then screw their brains out, all in the hopes that they have enough information they need to parlay that into a lifetime union. What people need to stop doing is feeling that if they push too hard, then they will lose the one who was meant to be in their lives forever. And the reason why is because if an individual is meant to be in your life forever, guess what? He or she will be in your life forever. Tricking, conniving or drugging this person will not ensure longevity. If this person is meant to be with you, then this person will be with you. By you and this person going through a certain level of adversity, you will ensure that the way this person is in your life is the way you want this person in your life. You see when people don't like you but continue to have sex with you and do just as much as necessary to keep up the façade that the relationship you are involved in is a real relationship, their interest can easily be swayed in the direction of another person. If all they are doing is fucking you, how easy would it be for them to say the exact same thing to some other loose moral having individual? For instance: 'I'm just fucking her but I really like you.'

Another one of the reasons or big reasons for why infidelity is perpetrated, is the one of people thinking that monogamy is not a reasonable expectation. Now maybe we are all not geography scholars and population experts but I am sure that all of us can and will agree that there are a lot of freaking people on this earth.

Recent estimates have the total at somewhere around or above seven billion. Now if this is accurate and there is supposedly one woman for every man, that would mean that there are at least three billion individuals for a particular person to choose from – give or take. With that being said, many people will fathom that with all of those people walking about, many or most of whom the average individual will never meet, what reason is there to believe that it is right or even feasible to limit his or her choices down to one? You see the thinking of some individuals is to spread the love, so to speak. They think that with all of these people on the planet earth, there is no way the meaning of life would ever include having sex with just one of them. The thing about this belief is that it is shared by so many people in this world – and the majority of the people who share this belief will never tell you. Many people often expect that when it comes to the perpetuation of infidelity, there has to be some far out, explanation of astronomical proportions of why it is committed but often it is as simple as a common belief.

One of the big questions people have regarding the signs of infidelity thing is how can you tell if your significant other is going to cheat? Now I believe that you can never truly tell for certain if the individual you are involved in a relationship with is going to cheat on you. But there are things, which are done in the beginning of relationships, which should give much insight. One of those things, and I tell people this all the time, is what happens when you and the significant other first meet. Does he or she show more interest in your physique than anything else? If so, then physical pleasure will more than likely be a motivating factor in the relationship. They will like you for your body and a pretty good guess is that they will like anybody else who has a comparable or better body than you. You see too many times we mistake someone liking what we posses for them actually liking us as an individual. It is the same thing with people who buy the significant other a lot of material items and the significant other likes the fact that he or she is receiving all of these things and mistakenly thinks that he or she likes the person providing these things. You see people motivated by a nice physique, will rarely be motivated by anything else – and this my friends, is one of the main reasons relationships have problems. Now this should be nothing more than a redundancy resource for most people. It should be such because many in this world should already know that some people only want you for the way your bodies are proportioned. Now knowing this, the question of who really was the one being deceptive when a relationship is forced after the fact of knowing the above? If a woman knows a man only wants sex and she gives in to him, is he wrong for leaving after he gets it? But see this is where that guilt trip comes in – under the guise of 'I fell in love after the sex and you should fall in love too.' You see, then comes the belief that we are now in a relationship on the part of one, which has not yet reached the consciousness of the other as yet. So when the other continues to sleep around, which is almost assuredly going to happen, the belief will be that infidelity has ruined the relationship.

Now let's just say that there was a committed relationship and it was violated because of infidelity. The thing about infidelity, which is confusing as shit, is how the occurrence of it will make the innocent victim feel that it is all the perpetrator will ever do for the rest of his or her life. You see, a man could cheat on his wife and they break up behind the occurrence. That same man could get involved with someone new or maybe even the one with whom he cheated on his last relationship to become involved with, and remain totally faithful. If he does, the thought will more likely than not be in the mind of the other that he will eventually cheat because he has cheated before. To quote a couple of women I have had the unfortunate pleasure of knowing, 'You ain't shit! You ain't never gonna be shit!' You probably gonna cheat on that bitch you fucking with now! And she stupid for trusting your dumb ass!' Now I will not bother to divulge who this individual was speaking to but it is obvious that the tirade was coming from a place of hurt.

People think that when an individual cheats, the only reason is because he or she can't help himself or herself and that it is all that the cheating individual is or will ever be capable of. This is where the once a cheat, always a cheat belief comes from. But like I always say when an individual cheats, either there is something wrong with that individual or there is something wrong with the relationship. A new person can have the tools necessary to fix what the previous relationship could not. And this is why people need to learn the individual they are involved with in a relationship and not just classify this individual as a man or a woman. You see using general tactics on a specific problem is a guaranteed recipe for failure. Some people think if there is no sex being had in a relationship, and somebody outside the relationship offers sex, then everything in the relationship will be fine. This is the problem. You must find out why there is no sex being had in the first place before you go and use new sex as the remedy.

A much overlooked reason for that of infidelity is that of respect. And by respect I am speaking of the respect of the significant other as a man or woman. You see, often people will discount everything that the significant other has to offer. Especially intelligence. What people will all too often do is get comfortable with the other in the relationship that they will think the significant other doesn't know anything. They will think that the significant other cannot offer anything except dick, pussy or money and aggravation. They will go to girlfriends and best friends and basically anyone outside of the relationship because they will be under the impression that whatever input the significant other has will be insignificant to whatever the other is going through. And this could be through relationship experience. This could be from stories, which are gender based, as in 'men don't know shit about women' or 'women don't know shit about men' and so on and so forth. What it could also come from is the much overlooked reason of there was little to no respect in the relationship to begin with. You see, far too often, people get involved with others for every reason in the world except love. They hope to grow into love. They get involved on the expectation of love and on the 'idea' of relationships. But far too few of them actually love the individuals they find themselves screwing. Now true, I believe that no two people in this world will have the exact same idea and or interpretation of love or relationships and what they both entail, but there must be a high level of equal criteria as a starting point. The idea of opposites attract when it comes to relationships is many times bullshit. Somebody who likes to cheat and somebody who finds cheating repulsive are what anybody in this world with half an ounce of common sense would call opposite. I want to know who in his or her right mind would deem these two types of individuals ideal candidates for commitment? You see this is why the criteria that people use for relationships is often sketchy. People have to examine and pick apart this type of criteria so extensively otherwise they risk involving themselves in a relationship with the wrong individual based on what others deem acceptable. In regard to the above example, you can be opposite but only so opposite.

You have to also ask is the opposite in mindset or is it just opposite in appearance, which attracts and keeps certain individuals together?

When people are suspected of cheating, the first thing the significant other wants to know is if they are doing it for certain. When people are caught cheating, one of the first things the significant other wants to do is get rid of the no good bitch or bastard. Now there are many ways to commit infidelity. And as such, there are just as many to detect infidelity as well. Focusing on the catching aspect, there is the hidden video camera to the straight up catching of the significant other in lies. Now as we all know or should know, lying about a member of the opposite sex is almost a guaranteed indicator of inappropriate behavior with that individual. But one of the simplest ways of detection is even before they have a chance to tell a lie and this is by being vague. When questioned about certain things or certain people, those in relationships will be as vague as possible with their responses to any questions you may pose to them. And the reason why is because they do not want you to know they are or may be cheating, duh. It is the same thing when people who speak two languages speak in their native tongue when in the midst of people who do not understand their language. This is done because either their native language is more easily understood or they simply do not want you to know what they are talking about. People are vague in many ways. You can for example, ask 'hey honey where are you?' And the wonderful significant other will say something widely accepted like 'I'm on the way home.' Notice how the wonderful significant other does not disclose his or her location. They will say their destination. And by doing so, they satisfy the question without actually divulging the information, which was requested. Genius! Many people who do not have deception or distrust in their hearts will easily accept this as a complete answer and the significant other, if he or she is dirty, will be free to do whatever he or she wants. If on the other hand the significant other is distrustful, then he or she can make the other disclose their location by using the tracking applications, which come standard on many electronic devices nowadays or by using video apps on their devices to see the significant other and what he or she is doing. People will say things to the effect of 'I just want to see your pretty or handsome face because I am not there with you' when in actuality they want to make sure that the other is where they say they are and doing what they say they are doing. The main reason people will use the vague tactic is because they do not want to lie to the significant other either because they feel that they are being honest by not actually speaking the lie or because the other is adept at understanding the signs that liars perpetrate. When an individual is vague, the interpretation of the answers given is up to the individual they are given to and if that individual interprets those answers wrong, it is his fault and not the fault of the other.

There are certain rules to relationship life that people must understand before getting involved, which will help make the transition from single to permanently connected much easier. One of those is the fact that no matter what is done during the relationship, the initial attraction which brings two people together will never be at the same intensity all throughout the relationship. The problem with this level of understanding is that even though most of the individuals whom are involved in relationships understand this concept, they do not know exactly when the change will occur. And that is the level of understanding that all people unknowingly desire. You see what we want in a relationship is happiness, and we want that happiness forever. If there is something that we do, will do or say that will upset the significant other or the stable nature of our relationship, then we want to know what that thing is way before we say, think or do it, so that we won't say, think or do it. The problem with this philosophy is that we will never know what is truly bothersome to the significant other until we do it. And no matter what type of relationship you are in or for how long, you will never know everything that bothers the significant other and this is because the significant other will never know everything that bothers him or her. If by some stretch of the imagination, one in a million, chance he or she does, then they will damn sure not have enough years on this earth to tell you. People have been trained or conditioned or whatever you want to call it to believe that as long as you continue doing what causes or caused initial happiness, that initial happiness will continue. I like to call this perpetual momentum. This type of thinking will place your relationship squarely on the path to failure. Quite often relationships are initiated on one thing. But never will one thing, be it the initiating thing or something different, be the cause of the relationships' continuance. And this has been shown countless times, through countless years, through countless relationships. If you start a relationship based on the appearance of someone, what is going to happen when they no longer look good? If you start a relationship on sex with someone, the prospect of or actual act, what is going to happen when there is no more sex? Or when the sex gets boring? (And yes sex can get boring.) If you start a relationship on lies, what is going to happen when that foundation of lies starts to break down lie by lie? You see what many people do is start a relationship on all the wrong things and then for some strange reason or another feel that the only thing which can fix the problems in that relationship is help from somebody outside the relationship – and the help that this

230

person outside the relationship more often than not offers comes in the form of sex. You see, sex is considered a fixer of all problems because too, too many people in this world equate or confuse sex with love. And you know the rest, love conquers all, yada, yada. But what people do not seem to realize is that sex is sex and love is something totally different. This is why when the act of infidelity is perpetrated, many times the one question, which is asked, rather demanded is do you love him? Do you love her? Nobody wants to ever believe that a sexual act means nothing more than a few minutes or hours of hide the salami. And this is because many people mistakenly attach the heart to the genitals so resolutely that they think there is no possible way to separate the two. This is why a one time act of infidelity will many times cause the end of a relationship. You see the thing about infidelity is that it manipulates the intelligence and interpretation of many individuals because of its' heavy interaction with feelings. People can have sex and not care about the man or woman they had sex with one bit. They can have relations with this individual for money and nothing else. They can have relations with this individual on a dare. They can even indulge in the little known act of pity sex. But here's the thing; these people can in no way believe that the significant other is capable of doing the exact same thing. This is the crazy hypocrisy about cheating. I can do it and it means nothing. You can do it, but it means everything. And this is in no way gender based. Men have relations with women they don't care about their significant others flip the fuck out when they find out. Women use a man for sex and their significant others wanna go and kill dude because of some guy code or because his man status has been challenged or some shit, when in actuality, all that has happened is an individual acted on his or her feelings or surrendered to impulse. But here's the thing: unless it is something, which is universally accepted, and by universally, I mean done and accepted by the entire world, how can anybody really be chastised for its occurrence. Infidelity is wrong by most accounts. Mostly because many people in this world cheat and they do it so much that they do not define it as cheating. In some countries, hell, in some parts of some states, people have sex parties weekly and monthly. In many areas, it is considered the norm to have as may sex partners as possible. In many instances, both parties are having relations with members of the opposite and sometimes same sex. So what happens when these people share their activities and or thought processes to those who find it appalling? Cheating is up to only the interpretation of certain individuals and the ramifications to it are up to the same.

Amid the massive amount of experiences and interactions a couple will undergo, there are two things I believe every relationship in this world will experience. They are the significant other cheating on them or the thought of the significant other cheating on them. Infidelity is so big, so common that an individual cannot go through life and not experience some form of it. And this is because there are scenes relating to being unfaithful or being tempted while in a relationship, in some form or other, on almost every television show you see. There is some form of infidelity or temptation in almost every song you hear. In so many of the books, which are overwhelmingly popular, there is some form of betrayal, even if it is between an unhappy couple and someone who will eventually become what the unhappy person needs to become happy. There is no denying that infidelity is a hot topic in the minds of people and on every form of entertainment. The million dollar question is why. You see, infidelity has always been wrong, which makes it exciting. People need excitement in their lives, even if it is the excitement of somebody else's life. Ever notice how someone can say 'look at her! She went to church 17 times last week instead of 14' and no one will give half a damn. But just let it be a situation of a penis being stuck into a vagina, which belonged to someone else and people start salivating. The problem with this world is that people are expected to be good.

And while good is at the end of the day, what everybody secretly desires in the person they choose as a life partner, good is boring. Nobody likes boring and this is one of the reasons infidelity is perpetrated or desired the way it is. I mean really ask yourself, have you ever heard of somebody being involved in a stagnant relationship going out to have an affair with somebody who is just as boring as the one the committed individual is in a relationship with? Now don't get me wrong, in some cases the above does happen but it is often gender dependant. Men will screw for the fact that they are able to screw. Women will screw to spice things up. Doubt that explanation? A man will screw a homeless chick. Women won't screw a homeless dude. See the difference. Now people will cheat because the very act itself will fall under the umbrella of exciting but as stated above often people will desire somebody who will excite them. Now the above is not a shot at men, saying that they will screw the random homeless woman who is talking to herself, smelling of urine, while simultaneously swatting away flies. This is to say that if a woman is in between homes, let's say in a shelter, more often than not, she will be seen as more desirable than a man in the same position. Another truth about cheating is this: the side partner will almost always look better than the significant other. The reason for this is because nine times out of ten the side chick or side dude has only but a couple of things besides looks and sexual capability going for him or her. The side dude more than likely can't cook that well. Neither can the side chick. The side dude is probably not the best caretaker of the children. And neither is the side chick. The side partner is probably good at conversation and hella good at sex but as far as the side dude or side chick being anything more than a great piece of ass, the chances are extraordinarily slim. You see if the side partner had any real relationship potential, the individual in the relationship who is cheating would leave the relationship to be with him or her. Meaning the side partner would be the main partner. But as we all know, the guilty party in the relationship will try his or her hardest to protect that relationship. He or she may not say it verbally but will show that the relationship is much more important than the few minutes or hours that he or she is giving to the side dude or side chick. Don't believe me? Then task the guilty party in an infidelity relationship, to lose either you (the innocent party) or the one he or she is sleeping with. It will be a landslide in favor of the innocent party. Now I am not saying that the guilty party should not face ramification for cheating, even though he or she is not in love with the one he or she cheated with. I am saying that often the attachment is many times little more than physical. The side chick is little more than a piece of ass. This is what one would call having the cake and eating it too. The thing about relationships is that there is often an unspoken ultimatum, which states 'you can have your cake and you can eat it too, but I'm the only cake.'

When it comes to cheating, there is one thing, which is prevalent, accepted and untrue and this is the excuse of 'it didn't mean anything.' This excuse is prevalent because almost all of the people who get caught in an infidelity situation will use it or they will use some variation. It is much accepted because it is just the right amount of pacification necessary to allow the relationship to continue. It is untrue because everything, which is done in this world, in this life, has a reason behind it. The question, which must be examined, is who does it not mean anything to? Is the meaning miniscule to the one who cheated, the one he or she cheated with or to the relationship? You see, if it meant nothing to the man or woman who cheated, you have to wonder how much does the sex act mean to you, the one in the relationship. You must also wonder if the sex act meant so little, then that would logically mean that the significant other would be completely capable of committing the sex act again and again. You see some people will open up a piece of candy and throw the wrapper on the ground. And why? It's because to them, the act is insignificant, it means nothing in the grand scheme of things. Nobody will or should even notice. Now apply that type of thinking to everybody else in the world: If we all threw a piece of paper on the ground because we did not value its effect on the rest of the world, pretty soon certain areas of the world would be overrun with paper. Now apply this type of thinking to relationships: if everybody in this world cheated, there would be no trust, no fidelity, no way to regard the significant other as anything more than a piece of ass. Now apply this type of thinking to the relationship which has been marred by infidelity: if there is little to no value placed on the act of sex, on the fact that the sanctity of the relationship has been violated, on the fact that the significant other may have been hurt beyond repair, the relationship will continue to be violated. The significant other will continue to be hurt. The act of sex will be little more than a man sticking his happy part into a woman or a woman letting a man do to her the same. Time to beat that dead horse. In the beginning of relationships, people get to know things about one another. This is the time in which people must find out about the major potential break up scenarios and causes. This is the time that people must discuss finances. This is the time people must discuss family. This is the time people must discuss if marriage is in the plans or if they will be just fucking for all eternity. And most importantly, this is the time in which people must discuss infidelity. You see the major problem that couples have nowadays is that they live according to a reactive lifestyle. In other words, when it comes to things like the above, they say 'oh we'll discuss it when we get to it.' Finances, they don't worry about until the bills are unable to be met. Family, they don't worry about until somebody ends up pregnant. The marriage thing, is not talked about in many cases, until years later and then when it finally is talked about, so much time has already been invested in the relationship, that even if the desired individual says no, he or she does not want to get married, the relationship will still be allowed to continue.

This excuse is accepted because it pacifies the significant other with the belief that he or she is important and the one who was used for the indiscretion was nothing more than a fuck toy. Now maybe this is true in the mind of the one involved in the discretion, but you have to ask yourself, do you want to be dealing with somebody who has that 'I do things on a whim because they don't really mean anything to me' mindset? Or do you want to involve yourself with that type of individual who is deliberate in every action he or she makes? AKA a thinking individual. Because here's the thing: if an individual actually sat down and thought about his or her actions, he or she would be aware of the ramifications of his or her actions. He or she would not just do things on the hope that he or she won't get caught. This excuse is accepted because people do things which have little to no thought behind them all the time and they use this fact to make the situation between the guilty party in the relationship and the one he or she had an indiscretion with understandable, and forgivable. You know if you really think about this, it is basically the equivalent of the impulse shopper mindset. It is commonly said that when people shop on impulse, they make impulsive decisions and justify them later. This excuse with infidelity is just that. 'I just did it' and the excuse, which will follow, is more than likely going to be completely reactive, and will come in the form of it meant nothing.

Now in regard to why many individuals feel the need to cheat in a relationship, the much overstated reason of not letting the other know about problems, which are occurring in the relationship, is one of the biggest. This is a fancy way of saying lack of communication. You see there are some people who will base a relationship on the prospect of sex alone. They will have sex and if the sex is good, will initiate the relationship because they think that they will one, always have sex and two, believe that the sex will always be as good as the first time. Here's the thing about that: sometimes people use sex as a trap to get others interested in a relationship. They will give as much sex, oral, anal vaginal, you name it, until the relationship is underway. Then the methods and frequency will magically and mysteriously begin to diminish. It's what we old dudes like to call the bait and switch. Give you as much as you want or need until you are locked into a commitment then KAPOW! No more nookie for cookie. Then what happens is the person who based the relationship on sex and nothing more will have no reason to remain interested in the relationship and he or she will go off in search of the thing, which attracted him or her to you (but from somebody else.) Then what will happen is everybody will surmise that he or she left a good woman or man for some floozy or some random dick because they were not ready for a real relationship or some other bullshit like that, when in actuality, this person was driven by a one aspect relationship goal and you, the innocent party, eagerly accepted. This is why you have to realize that when infidelity occurs, it is not only the fault of the individual who committed the physical part of sex with another. There are often things, which pull an individual away from his or her happy relationship and there are things, which push an individual toward somebody else. The big problem here is that many people do not think to examine these things until after the relationship is in serious jeopardy.

When it comes to infidelity, many times there is this ignorance, which leads people to believe that the only reason an individual cheats is because that individual does not love the one he is in a committed relationship with. This is not true in the majority of cases. Don't get me wrong, this does happen but it rare in comparison to the other reasons. People do cheat when they no longer love the individual they are involved in a relationship with. In fact women get credited for doing this all the time. They say men cheat whenever they can and women cheat when the relationship is completely over and they have little else to give but this is not always the case. Men fall out of love just like women do. And not only that, they initiate new relationships by having sex. People just don't fall out of love automatically. Just like when becoming involved, people don't fall into love just like that. The attraction may be immediate but the love aspect takes time to accomplish. The same thing occurs on the opposite end of the spectrum. The decision to end the relationship may be immediate but the things leading up to the decision can take years. Now I think most of us can agree that men are always the ones being given credit for being visual creatures and for wanting to screw before anything else. But – when the relationship is over in a man's eyes and he goes in search of a new relationship, and for some reason or other, the woman he is in the committed relationship with does not want the relationship to end or agrees to get back together and give it one more chance, the man will be considered a cheat and his actions will be interpreted as him just fucking some random bitch. You see people do not always cheat when the relationship is over or when they want the relationship to be over. They cheat for opportunity and often as an option for relationship correction. They do this secretly because they do not really want their relationship to end. They do it for excitement, for the thrill of finding out if they can get away with it. And proof of them not wanting their relationship to end is the massive amount of track covering they will indulge in to make sure that the significant other never finds out about the indiscretion. These people will cover their tracks like nothing you have ever seen – and this is the often hard to understand part. These people will risk everything they have for a few minutes or hours or days of pleasure, and then go through the most James Bond, Jason Bourne, any random spy tactics, to keep from getting caught and losing the relationship. My thing is, wouldn't it just have been easier to be faithful from the beginning? But there go people in their relentless pursuit of excitement, entertainment, relationship correction or stupidity, jeopardizing their lives and relationships, for reasons, which make little to no common sense. And on the opposite side of this reason for cheating thing, is the innocent significant other, who is under the impression that the only reason the act of infidelity was perpetrated was because there was love or some kind of affection involved in the transgression.

Another reason infidelity is perpetrated or what I believe to be perhaps one of the main reasons infidelity is perpetrated, is because people simply have no self control. It is the thought process of I can have whatever I want, whomever I want, whenever I want, that causes people to have problems with fidelity in relationships. A lot of times, not always, but much of the time, if you look back over an individual's life, you will see that spoiling children, giving them any and everything they desire can lead to acting in the above manner. And this is because raising them in this manner doesn't teach attachment. What parents all too often do is exist under the belief that for a child to be happy, that child needs to be inundated with toys and playthings. They make sure that a child has everything at his or her disposal and if he or she doesn't, then a suitable replacement is often close by. If the lesson of one thing is not to be valued, because you will always get more, as what is taught when you give a child whatever he or she wants, is taught, how hard is it to believe that that lesson won't be transferred from objects to people? There are many who say that if a man loves you, then he won't cheat. People say that if a woman is raised right, then she won't cheat. The one thing that we all have to do is stop listening to these well intentioned, ignorant ass people. Love does not always have to include a sex act to be valid. It is possible to have love for one person and have a physical attraction to another and not just have a physical attraction but act on it as well. Men and women cheat no matter what the significant other does for them or to them. True, there are unknown reasons, which will push a significant other towards infidelity but the bottom line is this: nobody takes a man's penis and forces it into a woman's vagina, except that man. And on the opposite side of the spectrum, nobody forces a woman to jump on the dick of any random man with whom she is not in a relationship either, except that particular woman. Now there will be those who will dress the self control issue up with common terms like boredom, emotional needs not being met, revenge and such but the bottom line is if you say you are not going to do something or you make a commitment not to do something and you eventually end up doing it, only two reasons can suffice as to why: one, you wanted to do it or two, you could not help yourself from doing it. Now here's the differentiating fact: the above two reasons are considered sensible and acceptable for every other action on earth, except infidelity. With sex being one of the most powerful forces on planet earth, some people still feel that everybody else should be able to resist the urge and temptation to desire it from more than one individual. They still feel as though sex is always about love. This is why some relationships will always fail. A saying, which is very prevalent in the relationship world is 'you may have a person's body and mind, but until you have their heart, you have nothing.' People who believe or live by this saying, will many times downplay the significance of any indiscretion which is committed as nothing more than a physical act and therefore should not be worthy of too much concern. As mentioned elsewhere, some people can say and actually believe 'the I love you, I'm just having sex with the other individual.'

One overlooked reason or not too much focused on reason for the act of infidelity, I mean besides the lack of control, lack of morals and all that other stuff, is one of the most basic. And that is the fantasy. Elsewhere in this book, I spoke about how so many people are raised on porn. They are taught that this is how people in the real world have sex and they are taught this because number one it is easier than going through the trouble of being completely honest and explaining about the problems of sexual incompatibility, sexual dysfunction and a whole host of other issues – as well as the fact that no one is actually going to let a young individual sit there and learn the act of intercourse by watching. So what happens, is the young person or the person who is not so well versed in the art of sex is going to follow what he or she is taught by friends or by what they see in movies or in the adult clubs. Now there are two things we will always see in this world. The first is what we want to see and the second is what actually exists. When it comes to how most of us are taught, there is no average. There is no a man or woman is going to be sexually attractive just by putting on a shirt and pants. What is taught is that an individual must fit into a certain level of attractiveness to be considered pretty or handsome and when they do, that is the time when it becomes acceptable for others to find interest. Here's an example: for those of you who have been to one of those strip clubs, have you ever seen a woman dancing on a pole, dressed like a housewife? And on the same note have any of you ever seen a male dancer looking like the much of the over 40 crowd, with the beer belly and thinning hair, walking around the club in a g-string? I don't think this happens. In fact I don't think it will ever happen. And this is because this is not what people want. This is what people have. Now granted, the above is no excuse. I mean nobody at the club is going to grab the dick of a married individual and forcibly insert it into another. The decision is always up to the one who makes it. But there are certain influences, certain temptations that propel others to do things, which ordinarily they might not be so quick to do. You see when somebody is dealing with an individual who is dressed the same way, like for instance, in a 2 year old scarf and a robe every night, gets approached by somebody, or not even approached but encounters someone on the total opposite end of the sexually attractive spectrum, do you think this person will be able to say 'no, this doesn't turn me on even a little bit?' Of course not. People are always going to be turned on by what it is that they are attracted to and many of these people are going to be tempted. Many people understand this. The expectation is that everybody in this world is supposed to always be able to resist temptation. This is what people do not understand. And here's where the division in understanding comes about. Many people will act on that temptation for no reason other than the fact that that individual satisfies the fantasy of what they secretly or even outwardly desire. Does it mean there is love for the individual for the fantasy? No. It means that there was one part of this individuals' existence that he or she felt needed to be satisfied more than any other and this is why people have to understand that a relationship is much more than sex – unless the relationship is nothing more than sex. That is a part of life. People fantasize about making an obscene amount of money. People fantasize about making love to their favorite movie star. People fantasize about traveling around the world and they even fantasize about that dream wedding. But there is one fantasy, which is almost never discussed and that is the sex fantasy. You see people fantasy about sex from the time they are very young. Much more fantasies occur once sex is had. Some people have fantasies about the perfect man or woman. Some have fantasies about indulging in sex with more than one person at a time. In fact the fantasy, which ranks high up on the degenerate scale for men is the one of having a threesome or group sex. Now what most often happens is these people who have these fantasies get involved with or marry those who are on the complete opposite end of the moral spectrum. In other words they will never allow the fantasies held by the other to ever see the light of day. So what is supposed to happen is the one who has these unrealized fantasies is just supposed to let them fade away into the sunset of his or her memory just because this individual is now involved with a 'good' man or woman. But you see sometimes it does not always happen like this. Quite often these fantasies never die. Sometimes they are just waiting at the surface of the significant other's memory for the other to do something that will piss the other off so that he or she can go and live out those dirty desires. Or there is always the case of alcohol, which is the number one excuse for people indulging in uncharacteristic behavior. There is always the 'honey it meant nothing. I just did it because you would never let me do it.' Is this normal? Yes. Is this accepted? No. You see people the world over are fully aware that fantasies, wishes, secret desires, whatever you wanna call them will be had by the significant other. The thing is that nobody is allowed to act on them if they present a plausible threat to the relationship. You see, sex has that type of power. Sex is believed to be the one thing, which bonds a couple together for life. It is believed to be the only reason love exists. The random individual will dismiss a relationship between a man and a woman if no sex was involved. This is why many times you will have somebody saying or asking 'do you love this person?' after sex was had or infidelity was perpetrated. A man and woman can be friends forever and say they love each other everyday. But as long as sex was not had, people will believe them to be nothing more than good close friends. Nobody will add the love title unless intercourse is being had or has been had. This is why people don't talk about the things that the significant other has or may have on his or her mind. The belief is always there that as long as those dirty and filthy sex fantasies stay compartmentalized somewhere in a deep, dark corner of the mind, they will not be allowed to cause any type of threat to the relationship if they are revealed. People figure that if you talk about what it is you really want to do, then you will have no choice but to eventually do it. And quite often this is the protocol for life; think about what you want to do, then put that plan into action. The thing about this though is that this boils down to the communication couples should have but are not having. Couples should be telling each other what it is they like and want to do before they get into long term relationships and then divulging those things after the fact. And the reason why is because after the fact is way too late. In the beginning, which by the way is the perfect time to find out all you can about what the other wants and expects from the relationship, you should ask these deep, revealing and possibly offensive questions, so that they don't surface later on in the relationship and cause all types of awkwardness. People need to ask what type of sex do you like? What kind of sex are you open to? What kind of sex do you detest?

And what kind of sex would you never ever consider? The reason why is because people have a habit of only divulging what they think the significant other wants to hear. They figure that when it comes to all of the wild and crazy sex positions and sex games and sex whatever, they will get to it when they get to it. But my question is what happens when you don't discuss it initially and wait several months or maybe even several years and then start talking about inviting another into the bedroom? The significant other will begin to think that he or she is stuck with a crazy pervert and will begin to act accordingly. This means that the significant other may begin to become inhibited and apprehensive about sex because the other is bringing up all of these wild and crazy ideas out of the blue. A person in a relationship who brings up these wild and crazy ideas later on in the relationship may scare the other into thinking that he or she is not satisfied with sex and that infidelity may soon be on the horizon. If this type of conversation was had in the beginning, then the individual would have had a pretty clear insight as to what kind of significant other he or she was possibly getting involved in a relationship with and whether or not he or she should run for the hills. Now people will say things like these demented desires should really have been discussed in the beginning of the relationship and I for one strongly agree. Tell people what you like and want in your life so that later on in the relationship, he or she will not look at you like 'you've changed!!!' I am not saying however that you should automatically assume that everybody whom you divulge your brutal honesty to will understand. You see, we human beings are the most understanding and at the same time most hypocritical. One second we understand that fantasies are normal and a part of everyone's existence. The next minute we are ready to burn you at the stake for having fantasies, which do not fit into our realm of normalcy. What this goes back to is the ever annoying and almost always avoided, getting to know part of the relationship. This is why in addition to being attractive and appealing to the significant other, an individual must be crafty and tactful enough to get across everything that he or she desires in the relationship, as well as what he or she wants and expects from the relationship, to the other, without scaring the other away. Now do you see why deception is many times the most preferred option? Society, the way it is, will never let the average individual, who has normal, bright eyed expectations of life, people and relationships, live according to those normal, bright eyed expectations because aside from everybody's expectations being different, everybody's expectations have been tainted. You see the way this world is, even the most vile and disgusting, heinous human being, will find something he or she does not like about how the significant other thinks. So often people have to understand the mind of the human being before they can go and say all men are this way or all women are that way. You have to understand what it is people have the propensity to do before you become involved. You have to understand that the mind has infinite, let me say this again, infinite capabilities, which are only limited by what one person decides to show you at any given time in his or her life. People far too often trick themselves into believing that an individual who does not divulge demented or questionable behavior is not capable of pulling questionable or demented behavior out of the air at the drop of a hat. I tell people all the time that the worst thing an individual <u>has done</u> is exactly the worst thing an individual <u>can do</u>. Now here's the thing about that statement: who is to say that the individual you are either in a relationship with or contemplating being in a relationship with will not only have but possibly surpass that behavior? People cheat because their minds are not correct. In fact people do most derogatory things because of the same reason. When people begin to act on the thoughts conceived by their incorrect minds, that is when they become dangerous. All fantasies are not bad. All fantasies are not good. The detrimental ones, the ones, which are hidden from much of society, compartmentalized in the minds of seemingly normal individuals, are the ones, which need to be focused on.

Why do people cheat? Short answer, it feels good. Well it feels good on the part of the perpetrator. The big, misunderstood part about infidelity is that those who commit it almost never think about how it is going to affect the one at home, the innocent party. In this respect, yes, cheating is a completely selfish and self serving act. You see there are some individuals who exude a certain desirability, which extends only up to and throughout the sex act. In other words, the prevailing thought is I just want to fuck this man or woman for no reason other than the fact that I want to fuck him or her. I guess you could call it some kind of raw animal magnetism that people for some reason or other cannot resist. The problem with this answer is that even though it is a very valid reason, most will never accept it – especially those who hear it after they have been cheated on. When it comes to infidelity, there are just two acceptances. If you cheat, you are bad. If you don't cheat, you are good. The problem with this is that unless you get caught in the act, confess, nobody knows for certain when infidelity is occurring or has occurred. And this is why many of the ramifications regarding infidelity are due to the thought, rather than the actual act.

People for the longest time have had different and varied interpretations on what infidelity is, from kissing someone outside of the relationship to having sexual intercourse with someone outside of the relationship. There are even some people who feel that if you talk about having sex or send explicit pictures to another who is not in the relationship, then you have cheated. But this goes back to the basics of the relationship. This goes back to the conversations that you and the significant other should have had about what constitutes a relationship and what constitutes infidelity. Unfortunately, people are still getting involved with one another because of ramifications, such as sex or pregnancy, and then trying to learn about one another as the relationship goes on. In other words, after the fact. You see if people were to lay out specific ground rules, as far as what type of relationship they will allow themselves to be in and what **specific** things constitute infidelity, there would never be anther argument about cheating again. But people don't do this. People never do this. And the reason why is because if people were to plan every aspect of their lives down to the who, the what, the where, etc. then the ones they would be in a relationship with would more than likely find them and the relationship predictable. And being predictable is about the biggest threat to happiness in a relationship. It is the epitome of one of those damned if you do and damned if you don't situations.

The crazy hypocrisy is if I tell you everything I need and want in and from my relationship, and we agree on the same points as far as what a relationship is and as far as what constitutes the act of cheating, then the only reason we would ever have to fight or become upset with one another is if you willfully decide to go against what you know I don't like. And then if you think about that from a logical perspective, if I know something is going to make you mad, then why would I do it? Sounds simply enough right? Yet the stats on relationships ending for reasons other than old age and death are still hovering somewhere around half (according to many of the relationship magazines out here.) So my logic tells me that people must want their relationships to end if they are going to do things, which would intentionally destroy them. Why else make these logic defying decisions? The reason why is because people in short do not know who they are fucking. They see something, which looks good and then they just go jump into the pussy or let somebody jump into them. And why? It's because they still feel that they have to be involved in a relationship before they get too old and don't have as many options. They go against every other rule for success because their hearts are involved. And see, these rules for success regarding everything else in life are simple and the same. They are learn about a situation before you go involving yourself in a situation.

Once you know about it you will have a much better chance at excelling at it. If people knew for example, that the average credit card charges 25% interest, they would not fuck with them at all – but see the thing is these credit cards look so good, appealing and are <u>easy to get</u>, of course people are going to make impulsive and wrong decisions. Then later on down the line, the regret comes in. The 'if only I would have known how you were going to turn out...' People always start to wise up when the pain enters their system. Now examine this from a relationship standpoint: if I know you are going to turn out a certain way later, then I will make sure that that way you are most likely to turn out is the way I want you to or I will avoid fucking with you in the first place. But people don't think in this manner. They get that credit card or credit card mentality, have all the fun in the beginning and then they wonder why cheating occurs later on. The bottom line is this: when it comes to cheating, many in relationships do not consider it cheating if they consider you nothing more than a sex partner. This all boils down to the interpretation thing touched on above. People are always going to have different interpretations on what a relationship is. This is the main reason why so many of them fail. One person may think I am just fucking you and the other may be calling mom to talk about how they found the man or woman of their dreams. This same type of interpretation is what goes on far too often in relationships where there is infidelity. People all too often get involved with others and believe that what they think about the state or status of the relationship is the exact same as what the significant other believes it to be. But far too often, nothing could be further from the truth. A person may just want to have multiple sex partners or as many sex partners as possible. And when an individual is looking to have as many sex partners as possible, this individual will say or do anything to accomplish that task. This individual will act like he or she is in a relationship. This individual will say as many I love you's as necessary to make the one he or she is sleeping with believe that the fake relationship is actually a real relationship. This individual will say as many I love you's as necessary to extricate himself or herself from the eye of suspicion of infidelity. In this individual's mind, it is not cheating if he or she just thinks that everybody they fuck is nothing more than a fuck partner. What he or she will say when confronted about infidelity is that it meant nothing and or the actual significant other is just caught up in his or her feelings.

The main rule in this whole cheating thing is simple. Don't have sex with anybody you don't want to marry. And the reason is because sex, whether you know it or not, whether you want to admit it or not, creates relationships. Now this piece of advice is for those who have deceptive intentions or who are not completely interested in a relationship with somebody when they go looking to have sex with this particular individual. People always wonder for example, how is it so easy for a woman to catch feelings after the sex act? I believe it's due to the fact that women are not screwing a man. They are the ones laying there while a man screws them. They are the ones allowing somebody to do something to them, while men are basically pumping away. You have to kind of look at this like one individual punching the other in the face. Even though they may both be engaged in the act of fighting, one gives something and the other receives something. The puncher always feels better than the one getting punched. In regard to sex, people say that both parties enjoy it equally and maybe this is true, but the fact that one is giving and one is receiving will always be different. It will always cause feelings on the part of the one receiving. Think again about the punching example: if a man were to go around punching people everyday of his life, what possible ramifications could he more than likely receive except maybe sore knuckles. Now on the other hand, if this individual were to get punched everyday, the damage would be more than external. This individual may begin to think that is all they are good for, just getting punched. You see men do not receive 'punches' and therefore will never fully know the impact of their interactions with women. So while the average man is saying 'here, take that!'

the average woman is saying 'what, that's it? You're gonna leave me now and I'm just supposed to be happy about it?' But you see this goes back to the basics of not only relationships but peoples' thinking and interpretations of relationships. Many men are out here thinking that all women want is some dick. They know that women will catch feelings after the fact but they figure if they tell the woman not to, then automatically she won't. The women are out here thinking that all men want is some pussy, so if they give the man what he wants, then automatically they will get what they want in return. You see this is where the whole hypocrisy, deception and game playing come in. If I know all you want is sex, then I can get all the things I want while giving you the promise that eventually you will get what you want. Or – if I know you want a commitment, I can just **act** like I'm in one because truthfully, how hard is it to have sex, and not talk to your spouse? As what many of the relationships in the world consist of today?

CHAPTER

~~12~~

Political Correctness Is Keeping You Lonely

PC. It is the abbreviated form for political correctness. It is the difference between pussy and vagina, ass and butt, politician and asshole. Now the difference is not always vulgar, as much as it is more accepted by more of society than the other. The term politically correct is more than a well placed word. It is many times a thought process. You see people are often their own worst hypocrites. And by this I mean that far too often the exact things they desire in this world are the exact things they will never achieve because those things are not presented to them in the way that they desire. People will say I want love but it has to be love according to my rules. There will be no deviation or settling. It will not matter what the other party in the relationship desires, as long as the needs of one are met. A prime example, or one of the most popular prime examples is how so many people in this world want to have sex and not a relationship, or a commitment but just a random sexual experience, will become highly offended when the opportunity presents itself. And proof of this is how is a random man, who may or may not be what the random horny woman is looking for were to approach the random horny woman with the following line 'hey, wanna fuck?' The random woman would more than likely smack the shit out of the other. But here's the hypocrisy: sex is what is desired! Now of course there will be those slight deviations in what is desired, such as a relationship, but for the most part, these people want to have sex. The crazy part about this hypocrisy is that you cannot like somebody just because – and this is especially true if you are a woman. This is one of the reasons why many men will say that women always like to control things or that women are crazy. You see it is not what people want, which causes headaches and difficulty and not getting it. It is how people ask for it. And this is why deception is so prevalent in relationships and general interactions. A person could easily say 'yes, I will let you screw my brains out' after being asked in the crass manner above, but this person will be looked at a certain type of way. She will be looked at as easy. But here's even more hypocrisy; easy is what almost every man in the world wants when it comes to a relationship. Very few individuals in this world really desire to go through problems to enjoy the act of sex. But people feel that they have to make things difficult to keep their self respect in tact. So let me see if I've got this correct; I want something, probably more than anything else I can think of right now, but I will not accept it if it is offered in any manner other than the way I want it to be offered. Is it just me or does that sound incredibly fucking retarded? This is one of the major problems in the relationship world. Everybody lives according to how society views them and their actions. In the scenario above, people would more than likely classify this woman as a tramp or easy or a slut, you name it. But what I have learned is that many of those who spew these hateful and undeserved labels are often envious and at the same time afraid to do what the woman is doing herself. Now please understand that I am not advocating that anybody go out there and be the spokesperson for free love by sleeping with any random dude who just asks for a fuck. I just want people to understand that society's opinions will many times drive your actions, and if a stop is not put to what society is allowed to do, the opinions of society will determine how you live your life and your relationship. In short, you will never know what it is you want out of life and you will subsequently never get it. The unfortunate part of life is that everybody is so concerned with this whole taking advantage thing. They are so concerned about being used and what everybody else will say if they find out what is going on inside their relationship. This is another one of those main reasons why relationships fail. All of this worry about what any and everybody thinks, is keeping others in their unfortunate and unhappy situations. You see there really needs to be some sort of clarification with the whole 'he only told me what I wanted to hear' thing or 'she only told me what I wanted to hear' thing. Of course they only told you what you wanted to hear because if they did the opposite, you more than likely would not have found interest in that person. I mean can you for one second imagine if you met somebody and he or she said everything that you did not like? I can hear it now 'I met this girl and she said or did everything to me that pissed me off but I still like her.' That right there sounds like a cry for medical help. People are supposed to make you feel good. I don't think that in the history of the world has there been a willing relationship, where one has treated the other any less than what he or she desired or deserved and the relationship was allowed to continue or be initiated. Now there will be some who will confuse the political correctness with morals but quite often, this is nothing but bullshit. If a woman were to meet the man of her dreams and she was horny as could be, the only thing preventing her from doing the do, would be her self imposed restriction or his delivery. And this is more proof that far too many times, we prevent ourselves from being happy for little reason other than the fact that we over think the simple things because of how others say we should be. Let's imagine for a second that there was somebody you wanted to bang into submission and the only thing stopping you from doing so and enjoying probably one of the best sexual experiences you have had in a month of Sundays, was you saying yes or no, wouldn't it really piss you the fuck off if you were forced into a decision that you more than likely would not have made if it weren't for the rest of society? But this is the power of the influence that society holds over people and their relationships. Now let's imagine if nobody gave half a damn about how an individual got their point across, just as long as it was respectful enough for that particular person. This world would be so fucking happy. But you see this world is so fearful of labels that to avoid being labeled, people will do anything to appease the powers that be. This is why people are not happy and this is also one of the main reasons relationships fail. Any physician will confirm that regular worry causes stress. Worrying about what people think is equally detrimental. Sometimes you gotta say fuck what people think. Sometimes you gotta say fuck your strong convictions. You see what we too often do is set the bar so high that others will never attain it and we unintentionally sabotage our own happiness. Then what happens is half our life goes by and we are not in relationships or we are not having the wild and raunchy, weekly sexual escapades that we dream of. What happens more than not, is our fucking years, you know the 20's and 30's will go by with us not reaching our full fucking potential, because we are so busy concerning ourselves with what others are thinking that when we reach the 40's and 50's, we have no choice but to lower our inhibitions as well as standards and act out with reckless sexual abandon. Then you start to see people fucking for no reason other than the physical aspect of it. You see while people spend all of their young years looking for the relationships and the sex but not finding it, so much time goes by that when they get older, they just say fuck the relationship just give me the physical, instead of the other way around. These damned labels are restricting this world from being happy. This teaching of no relationship is simple. This teaching of you cannot have sex and walk away happy is what is keeping people unhappy. To be able to say to somebody 'I just want to fuck you and I don't want to call you afterwards and I don't want you to call me, is probably one of the most liberating things in this world. No restrictions, no commitments, no attachments and most importantly, no expectations. Can life get any better? But you see, everybody in this world has an opinion and what's worse, everybody has an opinion about what you do. Those who fall into certain religious circles will have an opinion. Those who fall into certain moral compartments will have opinions as well. The thing about this world is that to be accepted as normal, you have to fit into somebody's opinion circle. And here's the thing about that: the less popular the opinion circle you decide to fit yourself into, the more you will seem like an outcast. And this is why so many people in this world are not happy. Now granted, there will always be something offensive or someone doing something, which is offensive to someone but instead of judging this individual and what he or she does, maybe we could look past that and say this crazy motherfucker is happy with himself or herself, and they are not hurting anybody, so just let them be. You see the bottom line with this whole pc thing is this: Either I have to be how you expect me to be or I have to be how society expects me to be. I cannot be myself. Think about that for a second. Everybody doing his or her own thing. Sure you would have people staring like you were crazy. Sure you would have people who do not like you. Sure you would have people wanting to hurt you because you do not fit into what they feel is normal but there are two things about this scenario many people do not realize. One: people would be so fucking happy if they did and two: this is how much of society is now anyway.

CHAPTER

~~13~~

Society Will Fuck Up Your Relationship

It is without question that maintaining a successful relationship is one of the most difficult undertakings in life. I mean aside from the fact that relationships are now being had between every type of individual, from man with man, to woman with woman, to transgender with regular to even transgender with transgender, there is the fact that almost no relationship in this world is only comprised of two individuals. The opinions of society, will many times dictate the course of your relationship and the reason why is because even though you may be wise enough to circumvent the bullshit that is being sent to you physically or even telepathically, your significant other may not. Your significant other may listen to the reality shows, the scorned exes or even tutelage from bff's, parents or maybe cosmo, to name a few – and bring that bullshit back to the relationship. You see if there was one secret for relationships to keeping them happy, then it would have to be the same as with every other aspect of life and that would be to keep everybody at a certain distance. We already know what happens when people input their two cents where it doesn't belong or is not wanted. Relationships become tainted. You see when one man and one woman are together, the relationship they have will be comprised of their desires, their thoughts, their dreams, goals and aspirations. The only thing that could possibly taint their existence is memories from the past. If however they listen to each other's circle of influence, aka mothers and fathers and friends and coworkers and psychics and whomever else, then all of those individuals will become influences and no matter how good the information these people give may be, the response from the significant other will more than likely be negative because you are no longer living your relationship. You are living according to someone else's relationship or someone else's idea of how a relationship should go. Here's my thing: you live and you learn. When you are young, you need parental instruction to shape you into adulthood. When you become an adult, parental instruction becomes a hindrance more so than a help. In fact, most outside influence becomes a hindrance to either one or both parties in the relationship. The instruction a couple receives should be from one another. The instruction received from parents and the above groups should be nothing more than a springboard to propel a couple into learning as much as can be learned about one another. But see this shows that people do not understand the power that just a smidgeon of interference has. Everything in this world will be changed if something is added to it. If you have a gallon of water and add just a little bit of cyanide to it, the entire body of water will be affected, not just the area which the cyanide was added to. Another example; if a ball is rolling down the street and you touch that ball as it is rolling, even if the ball continues rolling seemingly uninterrupted, and even if your touch is the slightest touch imaginable, you will still have interfered with the original path and destination of the ball. The same thing holds true for relationships. Once something starts, it will continue until it stops or until it is changed. This means a relationship will continue going good or it will continue going bad until it ends or until somebody decides to change it. People get all types of relationship instruction from everywhere. From parents to friends to psychics to even those silly assed reality shows. And I strongly believe that this is why so many of them fail. People who are in the relationship should be the only ones to allow the relationship to be ended or changed. They should know what it is that they want from the relationship and more than that; they should know what it is that makes each one of them happy. Once these things are known, the only other thing, which needs to be known is how to have these two things together with another individual. And that my friends, is what is commonly referred to as the getting to know part of the relationship. But this is also the part of the relationship where deception is at its all time high. There is no textbook time frame on the getting to know part of the relationship. People all too often think well you've known this person for this amount of time, you should this...and you should that...but what these people don't always realize is that sometimes it takes years to fully know somebody as well get to know if you really want to be with this somebody for the rest of your life. People change. People grow. They change from the person you kinda like into somebody you absolutely love. They change from somebody you kinda like into somebody you absolutely hate. If this chapter could be summed up with one thing as being all you need to make your relationship last, it would have to be an extension of the last few lines. Get to know the person you are dating, interested in or in a new relationship with as much as possible before you consummate that relationship. You see this is why some people never progress beyond a certain point. This is why some people never move out of low income housing. This is why some couples can never afford a car. They are too busy doing what others think they should do. They are too busy listening to those saying he should be buying you this and that. He should be giving you this amount of money every week. He should be...he should be...he should be...and this is not only a one sided thing. Men get a whole lot of fucked up advice from other people as well. Now the thing of advice, we cannot get away from. People will always be offering their two cents to those who don't want it. It's a part of life. Random people on the street will offer unsolicited advice for no reason other than the fact that you have not told them to shut the fuck up yet. But it is the taking of this advice and using it in your relationship, which is damaging to the relationship. Prime example: with the advice above, when others tell you that you should be getting this and that from your man or woman, no matter how self gratifying that advice may be, it will only be one sided. It will not be for the relationship. You see, people are so worried about getting pocket money instead of having relationship money. People want their significant others to buy them Gucci bags instead of putting that money toward buying a home for future generations. People want miniscule and miscellaneous items, like $700 phones but they don't even have that amount of money in their bank accounts to begin with and then they wonder why their relationships are suffering? Wake up people. When it comes to relationships, it is not about the immediate. It is about the long term. The goal should never be – be happy the first year and then miserable the next twenty. The goal should be get past as much adversity as you can early on so that the long term will not be adversity free but not adversity filled. This point cannot be stated enough: society determines your existence and the state of your relationships. Not you. You can say to everybody that your relationship is the best it could be or that your significant other buys you everything you want but if people will make their own decisions based on what they see. If, according to their criteria, you are less than happy, then you are. This is why you have to keep society the fuck out of your business. Society will tell you that your relationship is wrong because you are putting your man or woman before your kids. My question is this: unless society is living with you, your man or your woman and your kids, how in the fuck would they know? You see, the only thing society knows is what you tell them or what they interpret as being truth. The thing about truth is that it most often resembles a situation that is not fully understood. You see people cannot say to society my relationship is fine, my kids are fine, mind your business. And this is because people want to have a relationship, a family, and these nosey ass, good for nothing friends. And let's not forget about the rest of society. When people in relationships do not tell the last two groups about what is going on in their lives, the last two groups have nothing else to do, no other choice but to make assumptions based on what they see. And what they see is nine times out of ten not truth but a situation that they do not fully understand. And once this happens, these people will undoubtedly go off on their infinite quest to put their two cents into the lives of the other all because they think the other needs their help. This is very common and not so much of a problem. The problem comes in when the person in the relationship accepts that help and fucks up their relationship in the process. I have known people who have been in and are in relationships where they buy their significant others items of clothing which cost many hundreds of dollars but at the same time buy their children items of clothing which are not name brand. The prevailing belief is that they are putting their significant other before their own and taking care of the significant other better than their own. The thing about this scenario is that the significant other is grown and there is very little chance at changing him or his ways and desires. But the children are in that stage where they can still learn who to follow and be molded into what type of adult their parents want them to be. The children can still be taught that materialism is a choice, which can be made when you are grown but does not have to be instilled when young. Which brings us back to the point of you can love somebody but not what they do. You see, the prevalence of society's thinking will tell a woman that even though she earns more than a man, much more in fact, he is the man and as such, he should be the one to provide for her and the family. What this means is that certain women will not attempt to better themselves because that will be seen as her doing the man's job. She will stay in the same environment, stay in the same financial mindset, and keep the same friends who more than likely are the main ones telling her that her man is no good, all because in her way of thinking, her man is not doing what he is supposed to do. I mean think about something: if there is a couple where the man makes 4k a month and the woman he is involved with makes 10k a month and they are both unhappy with their living situation, what is so wrong with the woman going to the first real estate agent she can find and dropping 3k on a new nicer residence in a nicer neighborhood, and taking her man with her? Nobody will really know except her, her man and the real estate agent. But see, here's the problem: society has infected the thinking of so many relationships that if a woman does more for her man and family, than he does, he is less than a man. Society has infected the minds of people so much that the man has to buy expensive items to make his woman look good while in her unhappy situation. This is why you continually see people with 1k handbags living in low income housing and not that that is so much of a bad thing, as much as the fact that these same people are continually complaining about their unhappy situation. It's like 'yea, I know I live in low income housing, but at least I have a good man. Look what he bought me. He takes care of me financially.' And so on and so forth. It's funny; I always thought relationships were about a couple helping one another to better the relationship. But far too often, it seems like people in relationships are too concerned with helping themselves.

The Major Secret On Making Your Relationship Last

Wanna know the secret on making your relationship last? Of course you do. Everybody does. Here's the answer: there is no one secret. There are tons of them. What people don't always focus on when it comes to relationships is that a relationship is the immediate goal. A happy and lasting relationship is the ultimate goal. This is what so many people in this world fail to realize. One of the first and most important things to do is remove the word trust from your vocabulary – or if not remove the word, then remove society's overwhelmingly popular interpretation of it from your vocabulary. You see, trust is, in my opinion, probably the most over manipulated word in the English language. It is so manipulated simply because everybody in this world has a different interpretation on what it means to them. It is on the same level of over manipulation and interpretation as the word love. And proof of this is how if you ask ten different people the definition of love, you will more than likely get twenty different answers. Now the thing about trust, which is so detrimental, is the power that it has to dumb people down, so to speak. It will make the average person of average intelligence believe that what is clear, as day and right in front of him or her is only their imagination in overdrive. Trust is the number one enemy of common sense because common sense is 'I saw you in a car with the girl everybody says is a whore, and I know you're fucking her.' Trust is 'honey, I was just giving her a ride to the store.' And the significant other saying 'okay, if you say that's all you were doing, then I have to believe you because our happiness and our relationship depends on it.' You see, the thing about trust, rather the unfortunate thing about trust is that you need it to even begin to be able to call your relationship a true relationship. I doubt that the possibility exists for someone to be in a relationship and be able to say 'I love my husband or wife, I just don't trust them.' But yet many people do. And this is one of the major hypocrisies about relationships. People will be in them because they <u>need</u> the significant other, not because they trust them. They will be in them because they 'love' a certain part of the significant other or they 'love' what the significant other can do for them – but the total encompassing idea of loving that significant other entirely, this is the deception that many people perpetrate to one another on an almost daily basis. There is in many relationships today a thing of what I like to call satisfactory trust. This means 'as long as you don't do anything to upset the level of trust I have for you, then I will not have to look deeper into why I need to trust you.' Notice, this is not complete trust. This is adequate trust or an appropriate level of trust but it is not complete. We all know what complete trust is. Complete trust is unconditional. It is I will believe my significant other before I believe my best friend. Complete trust is I will not jump to conclusions without first giving my partner the benefit of the doubt. Complete trust is even if I see something with my own eyes, which has proven to be infidelity in other relationships; I will still give my partner a chance to explain. Do you see why complete trust is almost non-existent in relationships?

To give a relationship the best possible chance at lasting, one of the things you must not do is follow behind those who have been in relationships seemingly forever. And the reason is because nine times out of ten, those couples are miserable as fuck. You see the big secret about relationships, which last a long time is that no one will tell you about the bad parts. Grandma will never tell junior that she hates grandpa's fucking guts and that she's only with him because she is too old to attract someone more to her liking. The reason why she won't tell junior this is because she does not want to dash the hopes and dreams that junior may have of being the first person in history to have a perfect, trouble free relationship. That and the fact that junior will probably never be the same if grandma were to say some shit like this.

The second is to <u>extract yourself from the realm of expectancy.</u> This is exceptionally difficult because almost everything when it comes to relationships, is about expectancy. The expectancy of how a significant other is supposed to act. The expectancy of how a significant other is supposed to treat you. Even the expectancy of how a significant other is to be as a parent. But there is another part of expectancy that people have to be on the look out for. Too many people, both men and women feel that they are owed something just because they exist. Newsflash: the only thing you are owed in this world is the opportunity to make your life the best it can be. You cannot expect any man or woman in this world to take care of you the way you expect to be taken care of for one simple reason. And that reason is they don't know you.

The next is to <u>stop living according to everybody else's world.</u> You must make up your own rules for your own state of existence and live according to them. Now many people will say how can I live in my own world? The answer is simple. Make a list of what is important to you, not what is important to the world at large. We must stop with this whole female and male holiday thing. The truth behind the hypocrisy is that there are not holidays.

The truth is there are holidays for women and then there are holidays for couples. There is only one holiday or day of recognition for a man. And that is father's day – which if you really think about it, is really bullshit. Examining history, what really happens on father's day besides the over commercialization of the idea? People all over the city yelling out that annoying ass slogan, Happy father's day! Like it's really meaningful. Maybe there is a small amount of catering to the man but whatever catering there is will still be overshadowed by what is done for women. Don't believe me? If a man and woman were walking into an establishment on father's day and some nice person was holding the door for the two, do you think that nice person would jump in front of the woman to hold the door open for the man to go in first? I didn't think so. Then we have the bullshit ass stereotypical gifts that men get like the freaking ties and socks. Are you fucking serious? You give a woman some socks on mother's day and she will lose her fucking mind. Here's another for instance: Valentine's Day. Men the world over go damn near broke buying this shit and that shit for the girls of their dreams. And what do they get in return? Pussy. Now not that this is a bad thing because I honestly believe that that is the ultimate goal of many men and for some the only reason a relationship was initiated. But when you think about it, isn't this a little one sided? I mean the man has to go out and buy the traditional shit, chocolate and candy, and then what about if the woman he is dealing with is not the traditional type of chick? Then he has to go out and either buy her something especially for her or make something, which is only for her so that she can feel special on that particular day. And the way this world is, all most women have to do is give a man some pussy or maybe perhaps a blowjob or maybe even butt sex. Now again, these things are all fine and good but my thing is this: if we are having sex 3 - 5 times a week anyway, how is you giving me more sex after I buy you something expensive going to make me feel special? As far as the realm of expectancy, people far too often think and believe that they are always going to get something or be treated a certain type of way, just because they are alive. And unfortunately this is what many parents and commercialism have done to society. Because of these two, people are so into the 'it's my birthday, I'm supposed to get something. Or 'its valentines day, I'm supposed to get something.' And the real unfortunate thing about this is that these beliefs are so prevalent that they attach themselves to love. In other words, 'if you don't buy me something on these commercialized and highly popular days, then you don't love me.' Now we all know or should know that the above is not true but the problem is that since mostly everybody else falls under the magical spell of 'we get something because we are women then you are supposed to get something too.' And this happens to men so don't believe it is separated by gender. But my thing is what is so wrong with giving society the middle finger and making up your own schedule as far as when you want to make that individual feel special? What is so wrong with buying a significant other a car (if you can afford it) on April 21st as opposed to February 14th? I'll tell you what's wrong. Society says that you have to live according to their beliefs to be happy. And the ironic thing is when you live according to society's beliefs to be happy, most times you find yourself not being happy. Can you imagine for a second if a significant other came home one day in the middle of the summer to find a big ass red bow sitting on top of a brand new vehicle which was a surprise for no other reason than the fact that the other significant other wanted to do it? You see things like valentines day and birthdays are all fine and good if you want to buy a small token of appreciation or affection but my thing is why does it have to be only on one fucking day? If you love somebody everyday as most of these bullshit ass cards that people give to each other or birthdays and other special days say, then why not give presents and tokens of appreciation or affection whenever the fuck you want to, as opposed to when somebody says you should? This unfortunately is more proof that a relationship is not just about two people. Just let a birthday go by and nothing is bought. The girlfriends or family members will not hesitate to say how much of a fucked up man the significant other happens to be. These nosey buzzards will be so quick to surmise that there is turmoil in the relationship if things are not going according to society's protocol. They will say that the money, which could have been used to buy a birthday present, is probably being spent on another person, if money is the reason given for not receiving a gift. And this is not only limited to girlfriends. And this is not only limited to women. Family members love to put their two cents in when it comes to telling how you can improve your relationship. And you know what the bad part is? Too many simple minded motherfuckers listen. Sometimes, not all but sometimes, you have to cut the strings. And by this I mean distance yourself from family and friends and good intention having acquaintances because they will fuck up your relationship if you let them. Far too often, these people are not even in relationships but yet and still they are telling you how to run yours. Sometimes they are in relationships which are not happy and they see what has went wrong in their own relationship and feel that since they cannot fix their own, their tutelage should be nothing but welcome by you for your relationship. And you know what too many of us do? We figure that since a couple has been together for so long, they must be happy – and then we go off and follow the foolish relationship advice, which is given. <u>Society is the main perpetrator in relationship failure.</u> There are so many opinions both on the positive and negative end of the spectrum that people feel compelled to accept at least one of them when they feel their relationships are going bad or just in need of general help. The only problem with this is that nine times out of ten the people who accept this help cannot distinguish whether or not the help is actually good or bad for the relationship.

The power of society is often overwhelming, especially when it comes to who an individual should or should not be involved with in a relationship. Society will have you questioning whether or not an individual is a good catch if said individual is of a different race. Society will make you question whether or not an individual is a good catch if he or she has children from a previous relationship. Society will even have you questioning whether or not an individual will make a good partner if he or she has ever been incarcerated. In short, society has the power to make you question your own thinking power. Society will make you think that you are not intelligent enough to know what you want from a relationship just because the masses disagree with it. Now in regard to the above, there is a lot of race mixing going on. There are White people who deal with Black people. There are Indian people who deal with Asian people. In fact, there are people of damned near every race, who deal with damned near every other race of people. The problem many people have is that they don't have the power, which is needed to be able to say to the masses, stay out of my business. And the reason why is because far too often, we need those judgmental motherfuckers for some type of assistance. We need our families to run to when our relationships don't work out. We need our friends who will be there to say 'I told you so' when the person they told us not to get involved with starts acting exactly like how they said they would. And the reason these people are needed is because the ones in relationships are unable to carry on the relationship by themselves to begin with. There are going to be situations in your relationship, which are unfortunately going to be out of your control. One of those unfortunate situations is the one of your friends not liking or down right hating your significant other. This situation is reflective of not how much you like your friends or your significant other but of who holds a higher level of importance in your life. They will dislike the new or prospective significant other because they will feel that he or she is taking time away from family or friends. There are many who will reject the significant other or prospective significant other based solely on the opinions or approval of the friends. This, in case no one has told you, is bullshit. If you look diligently enough, you will find a reason to reject anybody in this world, from height and weight differences to color and religious differences. People will never find somebody exactly like them unless the individual they find is a twin – and even then, there are small noticeable differences. The one not so much realized thing about this world is the fact that people like whom they like. A person does not have to be anything other than alive to generate interest in the heart of another. Society will smash this logic to pieces and they will do so by telling you that somebody has to fit into a certain category for him or her to be liked. They will tell you that they must be providing you with this much money. They will tell you that the one you like must be this attractive. They will even say this person must be a member of this group, club or race. Tell society to stay the fuck out of your business. If people for one second stop to realize what got them interested in the person they are interested in, without the influence of society, many times they will settle on the reason as being nothing more than just having a general interest, like or desire to be with this person. Again, an individual does not have to be anything other than alive to generate interest in the heart and mind of someone else. If you really think about the main reasons couples break up and go through many types of adversity, you will see a lot of those reasons are due to other people. It's almost always 'he said this' or 'she said that' or 'he said you said this' or 'she said you said that.' The unfortunate thing about society, aside from the fact that there is basically no way to completely keep them out of your relationship, is the fact that they will always be trying to get into your relationship. You will always have somebody asking how's your husband? How's your wife? What do he/she do for a living? Are you two having enough sex? Are you happy with the sex you are having? And so on and so forth. People ask these questions, not for general concern but as openings to wiggle their way into your relationship. Here's the thing: you do not have to give them every bit of information to make them like you. Once people know about you and your situation, they can manipulate that information and use that information against you. I have seen it happen too many times. The best way to keep the door closed and not let them into your relationship is by keeping the door closed and not letting them into your relationship. Answer every question with one word answers. For example, how's your husband? Fine. How's your wife? Fine. How's the relationship? Fine. Sooner or later after unsuccessfully prying, they will stop asking. They will become upset that you do not share every intimate detail of what is going on in your life but here's the thing: sooner or later, they will say I respect the fact that you were always able to keep everybody out of your relationship. Sooner or later they will say you never go through any drama because of 'he said she said.' Sooner or later, they will say 'I wish I could be more like you.'

One of the last secrets on making your relationship last should be categorized as one of the first. It is what should be done when you are in the pursuit of your relationship. This secret, the one, which is the most simple and at the same time the most difficult, is the divulgence of complete, no holds barred honesty. You see too many people say 'I'm not going to tell my significant other I like to watch dirty movies and do inappropriate things with fruits and vegetables because it might scare him or her away.' They figure that they will just keep that little tidbit of information hidden or if ever questioned about it, they would just tweak the response ever so slightly so that it doesn't sound absolutely inappropriate. Here's the thing: what I have noticed through my years and years of dealing with and failing in many relationships is that there is no room for secrets or hidden desires in a relationship. And the reason why is because sooner or later, everything which is in the dark will eventually come to light. This means that it is very possible that your significant other may one day walk in on you sitting in front of the tv, watching a porno with your half naked body wiggling back and forth with a banana in some place I'd rather not mention. What makes relationships fail more than anything else are surprises and not the good kind. You see the good kind is waking up to oral sex. The bad kind is your partner having a threesome and using the excuse of honey, this means nothing, it was just something I always wanted to do. Here's the thing: if you tell the individual you are interested in what you want before the relationship commences and they decide to accept you regardless, there will be no surprise later of 'omg! I never knew you were such a freak!' and things like that. The bottom line is this: people expect you to be good, but they want you to have a little bit of bad somewhere in your existence. They just want it to be what they can handle and when they can handle it. When the relationship gets dull, then they want you to spice it up (but not too much.) Proof of this is how girls want to marry a good guy but who has a little 'bad boy' inside every now and then and boys want a lady in the street but a freak in the sheets. What the above basically boils down to is number one, knowing one's self and number two, being honest enough with one's self to admit what one may want down the line. You see, this way you won't have to deal with repressed fantasies and such. You won't have to deal with 'my life was unfulfilled because I never got to do this or that.'

When It's Time To Go

Out of all of the things in a relationship that people disagree on, there is one, which seems to have everybody in complete agreement. And that is the fact that there is no specific time on when to call it quits. In a relationship, people have one main goal. That goal is to make the relationship last until they get what it is they want. Some people want money from that relationship, meaning they want to be taken care of financially and others want physical pleasures, meaning they want nothing more than to give and receive the best sex they can imagine. And still for others, they want nothing more than to be in a relationship. These are all normal and common relationship pursuits. However as all good things must come to an end, there is a great deal of controversy regarding the appropriate time to end an unhappy relationship. Some people will end a relationship based on the fact that one unfortunate occurrence has transpired. Others will end a relationship because people outside the relationship will say that the relationship has run its course. And still others will end a relationship because they will feel that they have no other options regarding the relationship's continuance. The question I have is who is right? You see, just like there is no textbook protocol on when to start a relationship, the same truth exists for the opposite end of the spectrum. People meet, they fuck a week later and a relationship is created. People go on websites, meet somebody they know nothing about and the next thing you know they are in a relationship. So it's pretty safe to say that the initiating of a relationship is based solely on the individuals involved in the relationship. The difference about ending a relationship is that while people only get involved in a relationship one time, couples have been known to break up countless times before calling it quits for good. And in case any of you do not know, this is confusing as shit.

For a relationship to be truly over, the love, the feeling, which bought you two together, the thing, which has kept you two together, must be gone. Sounds simple enough right? Just feel in your heart that there is no more reconciliation, no more desire to work it out and wala! The relationship is over. But not so fast. You see, even if the relationship goes through all of the above and the last thing you want to see in the world is the significant other, he or she may be under the impression that the two of you are just going through a little something that you have yet to get over. This is the hard part – getting the significant other to believe as you do. You see the thing about relationships, which is really easy to miss, unless you are paying really close attention is that although the attraction, which brings two people together can occur at or about the same time, the hatred, misunderstanding or unhappiness is usually only one sided. This is what creates people becoming distant. This is what creates stalkers. Now with the whole distant thing, people do not have to become distant for weeks and months and years and years. An individual can become distant immediately and it may take the other weeks or months or longer to notice. You see there are many people in this who only have the ability to stick with something as long as the getting is good. In other words, if they are not happy with the situation or you, they can say 'alright fuck it, I don't want this anymore!' And they can stick to their decision, even if they never verbalize it. I mean people walk away from jobs without giving two weeks notice. They walk away from parenting responsibilities without giving any notice. So how hard would it be to walk away from a relationship, even if it is done only in the mind? Now think about that for a second. A person in a relationship decides that the relationship is over and begins to act as such. But this person realizes that he or she still needs something, which the other provides. So he or she stays around not reciprocating the love that is shown but just mimicking the actions of the other. For instance, one says I love you and the other says the same – not for any reason other than the fact that it was said to them. One significant other buys something for the other and the other buys something for the first. And not because he or she really put any thought into whether or not the other would be happy with what is bought, but only as a reciprocal action based on the action of the first. This is how easy fake relationships are perpetrated. There is no feeling behind the action, just the action. And if the other ever thinks about questioning the insensitivity of the first, they will more than likely be dissuaded by the thought that the first is just going through something, they have an attitude, they are just being men or women or one of the other commonly attributed excuses to how people sometimes act. This person could literally hate the guts of the other but as long as the other accepts the way the first is acting, the relationship may continue indefinitely. This is part of the deception, which is commonly carried throughout much of relationships. People say 'I don't love him, I need him' and they carry on relationships based on that fact alone. And people continue with this type of relationship because they feel that as long as they are being needed, they are being loved and their value to the relationship is somehow enhanced. But you see ignorance is what allows deception to continue. Now don't get me wrong because there are many in this world who know that they are not being loved but used for only what they can bring to the relationship – and they are okay with it. Many of these people feel that as long as they get to experience just a smidgeon of the complete relationship experience, they are okay with it. This smidgeon they are experiencing is the same as what is commonly known as a one aspect relationship. That one aspect could be sex. It could be money. It could even be just having the ability and privilege to be in the presence of the other. Yes some in this world are needy like that. And yes, this is the equivalent of a completely fake relationship but too many live according to this manner. Now for those who are not needy or hell bent on making the other's happiness their ultimate goal, with no regard for their own, situations such as the above, clearly show a need for the relationship to be over. If that's not enough, then when the significant other can no longer make you happy and you no longer want him or her to try should be the time that you and him or her call it quits. Unfortunately, some people feel that the only way out of a relationship is death, meaning they do not believe in divorce or any other type of man made separation. Many outsiders, who have no idea of your situation, will try and tell you that you should trick yourself into staying where you are no longer happy. They will tell you that you should work on it and give in to the others' demands and requests. I say fuck that. But that's just me. If you are in a relationship and you are unhappy, you should first try to get your partner to make you happy. Second, if your partner cannot make you happy, you should really question why you are in the relationship at all. Third, you should simply leave that shit. Now of course there will be many people who will say that relationships should be preserved at all costs. I believe a little differently. I say that <u>happiness</u> should be preserved at all costs. I mean correct me if I'm wrong but I don't believe anybody wants to be able to say after years upon years of being together that 'this man or this woman took care of me well but never made me happy.' This is the same thing with the job where the benefits are stupendous but you can't stand the work. Do you suffer for twenty years to be happy after? I think not. Peace of mind is so undervalued but so extremely important in life, in the workplace, and in relationships, that without it, people will die. And this occurs by them stressing themselves out so much trying to make the other(s) happy that a heart attack occurs or they can't take the pressure from the other(s) so they go get a weapon and put out the lights of the other and themselves. This is why it is said that marriage should not be entered into lightly. You see the idea behind marriage and relationships is that you have to become involved with somebody you don't really know and then stay involved with them for the rest of your life. Is it any wonder so many are unhappy in those long term unions? Is it any wonder why people after a certain number of years see each other and don't smile. It's like 'just get in the car and don't say anything.' You know, that type of attitude. It's like people have a perpetual mean and evil streak when it comes to being around the significant other. It is a total 180-degree turn from when the two of you first got together and every time you would look in each other's eyes, you would smile, but now each time you look in each other's direction, the entire disposition changes from 12 in the afternoon sunny to 12 midnight dark. The thing that many do not realize is that for ***happiness***, you need to know somebody ***explicitly*** and this does not always just take one or two years. If life expectancy for most people, is say around seventy, eighty or ninety, is the choosing of someone for all of those years after knowing them for all of one or two really the most feasible decision an individual can make? Now sure people will say that a relationship is all about learning each other. You know the ole 'relationship is the journey, not the destination' thing. But my thing is this: wouldn't it be better to know as much as you can about an individual before getting involved and having to live with years of regret? There is <u>no</u> textbook timeframe on how long it takes to appropriately get to know somebody or to groom him or her to your specific liking. Sometimes it takes years, sometimes many years in fact until people are comfortable enough to say they actually know one another. But no matter how long it does actually take to get to know somebody, once the bell has tolled and it's time to go, then it's time to go. Stop with this whole 'maybe I should give him or her one more chance because they were good to me in the relationship and he or she is really a good person deep down inside and they are just misunderstood' bullshit. This thinking is the type of shit, which will have you trapped in your emotions until the end of time. This is the emotional roller coaster that people talk so much about. This is the way people manipulate your feelings. They treat you like shit, then when you get tired of being treated like shit and decide to leave, all of a sudden they learn how to act right and how to treat you how you should be treated. That's real convenient isn't it? Then, after a certain amount of time, these people start acting the fuck up again and you get tired of it again and decide to leave and then they start acting right until you come back and so on and so on. Fuck that shit. A relationship should go as follows: instruct your significant other on how you wish to be treated. If they understand, continue on in the relationship with them. If they deviate, maybe give them one more chance but no more. Once people know what you want, they then know what they have to do to make you happy and subsequently keep you. If they say they can do it but know in their hearts that they can't, they are liars and they will eventually be found out. But here's the thing: if you keep giving chances for others to get it right, you will never be happy. The choice is yours.

This last part, I honestly believe goes without saying; violence, whether it is the physical or emotional kind, is definitely the time quits should be called regarding a relationship. But you see what far too many people do is look for the good in the other person. They accept things like 'I didn't know what I was doing, I didn't mean to do it and I will never do it again.' And with these acceptances, the relationship is allowed to continue and so is the opportunity for the violence to occur again.

Commitment vs. Living Single

In the ongoing debate about whom is happier, single people or those in relationships, there are certain positives and negatives on both sides, which must be considered. On the side of commitment, the first and major perk is that of commitment. You have somebody who has given his or heart to you with little more than the expectation of the same. You have someone to devote your life to. You have someone to worry you sick when they don't call all day and someone who will do the same for you.

When it comes to living single, many people will argue that the one perk, which seems to trump everything that the commitment end of the spectrum holds, is the fact that since you are single, you can do anything that you want to without the worry or pressure from anybody else to hold you back. This means that if you wake up on Monday and you feel like traveling half way across the world, you can. This means that if you desire to have relations with ten members of the opposite sex, at the same time, you can. This means that if you want to stay secluded in your home for a week straight, without calling anyone, without changing your clothes, without doing anything other than peeing and eating, guess what? You can. You see the thing about being single, which is highly desirable, is that as long as your actions are legal and for the most part moral, there is no limit to what you can do. You do not have to answer to anybody. And then people want to wonder why so many shy away from the idea of commitment. There is a common saying, which goes commitment is fine if you have the right person. And I must say that I am somewhat inclined to agree. But here's the thing: how many people find the right person on their first try? You see, the too much repeated comparison about relationships is that they are something like a job interview. This is incorrect. Relationships are <u>exactly</u> like a job interview. Think about something: if any company or organization hired everybody or anybody who came to apply for the position, the chances of that organization succeeding would be slim to none. This is why businesses have interviews. They have to get a feel for the individual who will work for and represent the company. They have to deeply examine and filter out the bullshit, which is cleverly concealed within the resume. When it comes to relationships, it is much the same thing. People have to examine your past. They have to see if you will be a good fit for them. They have to find out what you have to offer and if you will represent them in a positive manner. You see, this is why so many people like, no let me rephrase that. This is why so many people love being single. You do not have to put up any fake front like you are the best candidate for the position. You do not have to continue to strive to be the best you can be to keep the position. You can have the attitude of this is me, take it or leave it. If you don't like it, I will move on to the next available position or next available person. The major problem in relationships is that too many committed people carry along the single person mindset. In other words, I am supposed to act like I am concerned but in all actuality, I really couldn't give a fuck. You see this is why when relating to business, people who have the single minded mentality, care very little about anything other than keeping the position they presently have. This means that they will do just enough to keep that position. They will go through ups and downs to the effect of whenever it seems like they are in jeopardy of losing the job, they will work harder and more diligently than throughout any other part of the relationship. And this is so that the powers that be will be under the impression that they really care about the job and will do anything to keep it. This is the same thing, which is perpetrated in a lot of relationships.

People will act like they do not care right up until they are in jeopardy of losing their relationship, then it will be all I love you this and I love you that. I will do anything and whatever it takes to make sure that you do not leave me. Ain't this some bullshit?

Commitment is a lifestyle change. It is a lifestyle change because simply no one is born into it. People are born by themselves, not married, not in relationships, but by themselves. They have years upon years of practice in being single and then when looking for a relationship, they must forego all those years of practice in doing the opposite of what they hope to do for the rest of their lives. It is not easy. But the highly controversial thing about this thing of making this lifestyle change not being easy, is that it is expected. And not only is it expected, it is expected without deviation. This means that no matter how many men or women you may have been involved with, had relations with, or just found an unexplainable attraction to before you decided to involve yourself in a committed relationship, all of that shit has to be forgotten – and quickly. Almost as if it had never happened. When the average person looks at things from a different perspective he or she will see that this is almost impossible to do. This going cold turkey if you will is something that human beings are not equipped to handle. People are not taught indulge in something all of or most of your adult lives and then stop without ever longing for it again. People are taught when you indulge in something for an extended period of time; it will be that much harder to wean yourself off of it. Look at how people who are addicted to cigarettes break the habit: they have support programs, so that they do not fall back into the pattern or temptation of smoking. They have patches to curb the desire for the habit. They have all types of things to aid the individual trying to make that lifestyle change. They do not pull cigarettes out of the person's mouth and say 'you can never smoke again' and expect the person to number one, not smoke again and two, not be tempted, especially when the availability of cigarettes are basically everywhere you look. It is the same thing with a baby and a bottle. You do not take the bottle away from the baby without a suitable replacement. There is a bobo or a pacifier to take the place of the bottle. The way that everything else in life is, is catered to easing somebody into a new venture. It is not just throw this individual into the water and see if he sinks or swims. The only difference is that when it comes to relationships, this is how people are expected to be. And this, my friends is one of the main reasons why they fail. If an individual is not ready for commitment, how in the hell do you expect an individual to excel at commitment? People say all the time that when an individual has had several relationships, that he or she is used up or jaded or full of baggage. I tend to disagree somewhat. Individuals going through certain relationships, while possible grasping the opportunity to acquire baggage and negative feelings toward the opposite sex, will also grasp the oh so necessary experience in what it is he or she wants, does not want and will or will not accept from the relationship. You see, to excel at anything in life, you need experience. Relationships are no different. You just have to be able to decipher who is well versed in relationships and who is a slut. You have to be able to decipher who is running game and who is sharing his or her years of experience with you. The thing about mostly every relationship in the world is that the participants basically want two things. The first is good sex and the second is no problems. When in the single mindset, there are very few problems and this is because the relationship goals pertaining to single life are relatively simple. When you are no longer single there are many times more arguments and why? Simple, you have more things to argue over. You have kids, you have bills etc. The good sex and no problems is basically the blueprint for single life. The main difference between the two is related to age and or maturity. When people are young or are of that young mindset, they will act and live reckless. They will have wanton sexual escapades with as many and as often as they can. When people become older or mature, things like sleeping around and related activities lose their status of importance. The focus then becomes holding on to one relationship and making it the best of all the others. The problem with this understanding is that just because people become older, that does not mean that they have achieved wisdom. Some full grown men and women are still sleeping around like the reckless teenagers they once were. And some young people are in seemingly lifelong relationships. So the case for commitment vs. single can very well boil down to a case by case basis.

One of the biggest areas of detriment that an individual can cause to himself and his partner is that of confusing longevity with love. Longevity basically means long life or in this instance, long relationship life. What people will do is live under the belief that every relationship is automatically growing and progressing in the manner that they not only want it to but expect it to just because two people are involved in it. They will continue to believe that the longer you or a couple is together, the more love there is in the relationship. This right here is the total power of deception at its finest. Society and its often twisted interpretations of life's interactions, will say that because you screw somebody for a few months or few years, then you are a couple and not only that but a loving couple as well. But here's the thing that everybody walking the face of this earth should already know: a person does not necessarily love you just because he or she stays in a relationship with you for an extended amount of time and does what other people in relationships do. I mean how hard is it really to mimic what people in loving relationships do? All that is necessary for a fake relationship to exist is for the participants involved to have sex on a regular or semi regular basis, give each other money and **act** like there is genuine concern for each other's existence. People can do the above stated actions for years upon years and here's the kicker: none of these stated things involve love. I mean a couple can say they love each other but couples stay together for years and the love is never shown. It is never proven. It is only spoken. And the reason why is because these people have different interpretations of love. Some of these folks believe that as long as the significant other comes home every night, that that small action is representative of the amount of love, which is held for the significant other. Some people will use the 'I don't cheat on you' reasoning as evidence of love. And there are those who speak the words 'I love you' and not only that but throw around the fact that they say those words to the significant other all the time, as proof of their love. Again, none of these are representative of most of society's interpretations of what love entails but these are some of the things that many in relationships accept.

The Bullshit About A Break

There is no such thing as a break unless it is after the fact. An individual cannot plan for a break. It just doesn't happen. What happens all too often is a couple will reach that point of indecision, that point of I want to let you go but then again I don't, that point of I just want the pain to go away. And when couples reach this point in their relationships, nine times out of ten, they are not prepared to handle it from a logical perspective so what they more than do is respond to the unhappiness they are experiencing impulsively. In other words, they say things to the effect of 'let's take a break.' Now had this been a situation of the two individuals in the relationship being involved in a boxing ring instead of what is supposed to be a loving relationship, the idea of a break would be fine. You know the ole go to your respective corners and regroup, catch your breath, yada, yada. But see this is not a boxing match and far too often that when a break is suggested, it is not always a shared intention to come back refreshed, with renewed vigor to continue on in the match. It is often a one sided belief that the relationship is over or if not over, then the break is seen as a permission slip to live single until the break is over. In the grand scheme of things, we all know what this is. That word we love to hate, communication – rather the lack of. You see, since a break is little more than the impulse reaction of one or two individuals who have no other immediate options at the time, people do not impose restrictions or stipulations on what the break entails. The only thing, which is relayed to one another besides the fact that a separation is imminent, is the expectation that each other understands what the other wants. Do you see how this creates problems? I say to you that I want to be away from you with the expectation that we will work on each other or the relationship and then when either you or I or both of us feel that the relationship is at a place where we can successfully carry on, we will get back to the relationship with full force. You on the other hand, stop listening after I say I want to be away from you. The really unfortunate thing about relationships is that people live under this expectation of equality when they are in relationships. They think, no wait – they honestly think that the other not only thinks as they do but does as they do without the other having to tell them. You see, this is why relationships fail. People, as smart as they are, as technologically advanced as they are, as Ivy League educated as they are, are many times dumb as donuts. You have to tell others what you want them to know. In addition to people being dumb as donuts, many of them have this short term deficiency thing attributed to them where they can only remember what you say for a certain amount of time. Now this is not to say that it is okay to nag and beat somebody over the head with what they have done when they have done something wrong. This is to say that many times you may need to reiterate what it is you want, need and expect from the significant other, to the significant other.

Now what people do in these 'break' situations is live under two separate ways of thinking. As stated above one will be under the impression that the relationship is over or ending and will act accordingly. This individual will begin to seek out other relationships, which may be sexual in nature or may look for a permanent replacement. This individual may just develop in his or her mind, a way of thinking which even if the two who are on break get back together, will resonate as him or her being left at one time and is therefore single. This individual may think that you left me once and you may do it again under the guise of this break thing, so I will protect my heart by remaining single in my mind, even though we are together in the physical sense. This individual, may, as stated above get somebody pregnant or become pregnant while sleeping around either in search of a new relationship or as a way to heal from the hurt caused by him or her thinking that the break was permanent. When the break is over or when the fact that a child was conceived is revealed, the relationship which should have been on the road to repair, will have to face new adversity because the one who either initiated the break or who just needed to examine where the relationship was heading will believe that the other did not want to continue in the relationship and this is why this individual started sleeping around. Now the other individual is the one who is truly undecided about where he or she wants the relationship to go.

That Relationship Which Is Purely Sexual

Under the umbrella of living single, people will undoubtedly desire a relationship, which contains little more than the occasional bump and grind. This is pretty much protocol for those who are not yet looking for a relationship, but want to enjoy the perks of such. Now there will no doubt be those who are in relationships already but still want to enjoy the perks of living as if they were single also. These people, the cheaters, are the ones who are bad. They are the ones screwing up those nice guys and nice girls for all eternity. Now what makes the 2nd group bad is that they outright cheat. What makes the 1st group bad is that they let the others believe they are in a relationship, and then when feelings start to creep in, they pull the proverbial rug out from under their feet, so to speak. Now a purely sexual relationship is what is desired by much of society, whether they admit it or not. And the reason why is because sex is usually the one thing, which makes an individual feel good each time it is done.

When it comes to relationships, people generally want two things. The first is good sex and the second is no problems. This is one reason hookers will never go out of business. This is also one reason why relationships will always end due to infidelity. Now true many people desire the related things in relationships like support, and talking and walks in the park, date nights and yada

yada, but the main things, which drive the preponderance of relationships are the top two stated above. When people are involved in these types of unions, they must not do the one thing, which has proven to be detrimental to every other friends with benefits relationship in existence and that is crossing the boundary of two people who have sex and two people who have sex while sharing feelings. When feelings come into the relationship, whether it is on the side of one or on the side of both, you have the makings of a relationship. One of the biggest things people say to the other party in a friends with benefits situation is don't catch feelings, don't catch feelings, don't catch feelings – but many times the act of sex is much more than just bang bang bang bang bang, as John Witherspoon from The Wayans Bros. tv show would say. You see what people have to do, just like when dealing with an ex lover who cannot seem to get the message that the relationship is over, is be cold toward this person at all times except when indulging in intercourse. The only difference with the ex is that there will be no more intercourse and instead of being cold, mean is more the operative word. What people do not seem to realize is that a purely sexual relationship, is sex, without the relationship, just like a regular relationship, only without the sex. Which means that if you do everything besides sex, then you may trick yourself and the other party into believing that actual feelings of love and whatever else that a real relationship would have, actually exist. So to avoid any confusion, if the relationship is going to be a purely sexual one, the only thing you should be doing is having sex. You should not be calling to see how his or her day was. That's what people in relationships do. You should not be sending funny texts back and forth. That's what people in relationships do. The only thing you should be exchanging is bodily fluids (protected of course) and the reason why is because if you or your partner do any of the above stated things or more, you will be venturing into relationship territory. You will be doing things that people in relationships do and the next thing you know, you will start to think of the one who was supposed to be nothing more than a sperm receptacle or sperm depositor as a concrete, living being, who is worthy of being considered good enough for an actual relationship. Do not allow yourself to think about his or her good points or positive attributes. When you do, the fantasy becomes real. The fantasy is supposed to be the best sex, with no problems you have ever had. When the fantasy becomes real, the opportunity opens itself up for problems in the form of feelings of attachment, jealousy when somebody else comes into the picture, and more. With the purely sexual relationship, there are no expectations and there should be no disappointments because both parties know that a fuck is the goal. Nothing more.

Now the thing about the purely sexual relationship, which people all too often overlook, is the fact that it is rarely a purely sexual relationship between two single individuals. More times than not, either one or both is involved in the relationship because the sex is not on the level of what one of both of them want it to be. Many times these people in purely sexual relationships have significant others at home who are good in every way except the bedroom – and the purely sexual relationship (psr) allows for every type of experimentation and fantasy imaginable. The thing about the psr, which is not only bad but detrimental, is that sooner or later the feelings which are shared will if not careful eventually parlay themselves into love. This is bad because even though many, many relationships are started in this manner, it is not always possible to rid one's memory of how the relationship began. You see what many people do when they are involved in relationships is have a secondary relationship if the initial relationship is not living up to their interpretation of everything that a complete relationship should. In other words quite often it can be a situation of 'I have a husband or wife, and I have a side man or side woman for everything that the husband or wife cannot provide.' What many times ends up happening is that the 'side person' ends up becoming the main person and later on down the line, the thoughts of how the relationship conceived itself will resurface – either on the part of one or one the part of both. The thought will many times be 'when we met, you cheated on your last relationship, so number one; you are not completely trustworthy and number two; what guarantee do I have that you will not cheat in the present relationship? Now this belief does not have to be spoken to exist. You see, no matter what people in relationships may tell the significant other about always speaking their mind and not ever holding on to things without letting the partner know, nobody in a relationship is going to tell you everything that he or she is feeling, doing or especially thinking. Now the controversial thing about this is that this is not a thing of getting to know the other person. This is a thing of getting to know the other person's mind. This is impossible to do. It is impossible to say I know what you're thinking. Or I know how much you respect me in this relationship and as a person. Or I know that you will not hold on to my past and bring it up later on in the relationship to use against me. You see people are so deceptive. They will lie just to get into a relationship with you. But here's the really bad thing: sometimes people are not deceptive at all. They just cannot handle everything that goes on in a relationship – and in regard to the example above, an individual could have tried his or her heart out to move on with a relationship after meeting in the unorthodox manner shown but may not have been able to rid himself or herself of the fact that at one time in your life, you were not trustworthy. And this thought may linger in an individual's mind for the duration of the relationship, even if you were able to forgive this person and move on as if nothing inappropriate had ever happened.

Texting And Sexting While In A Relationship

When I was young, there were nudie mags. As I grew up, there were nudie mags. In fact, as far back as many of us can remember, there were nudie mags, so this whole thing of naked pics, is not in anyway new. People have been interested in the naked body for eons. As of late however, there has been this whole thing of not only taking naked pictures but taking and sending those naked pictures all over the information superhighway. It happens so much that it has been given the name sexting. Now this is the new hot thing causing detriment in relationships because even though people have been admiring and taking pictures of their bodies for about as long as most can remember, sending those pictures instantaneously is almost a guaranteed admission of guilt. If it is not an admission of guilt from the one sending the flicks, then it is damned sure a presumption of guilt from the one who catches the other sending those pics. I mean think about it; what reason in the world could there be for sending a picture of your penis or vagina to a member of the opposite sex, unless that member of the opposite sex was a member of the medical community? There is no denying that this is either an invitation to infidelity or an extension of. It is not one of those easily mistakable situations like just being in the presence of the opposite sex without the significant other or having the opposite sex's number in your phone. The thing about this action is that even if it is done as a joke, as what teenagers do or a disrespectful and vulgar act, as what scorned people may often do, the significant other will always assume that it is being done to initiate a sexual relationship some people and their interpretation of things will instantly label this act as cheating, even though there was no actual physical contact involved. And this again is one of the reasons why you and your partner alone, not you, your partner and the rest of society, must figure out what actions are wrong, bothersome or detrimental to not only the significant other but the relationship in general. Relationships are made and based on the assumption that whatever the majority of society likes or dislikes, will be what your significant other must like or dislike as well. This, coupled with different interpretations, will continue to cause relationships to fail worldwide. You have to not should but have to understand and agree with how your significant other thinks before you get involved with him or her. Otherwise, mistaken or not completely understood situations are going to destroy any chance at happiness you can ever think of. if I could give some advice based on my vast experience with this topic, it would be: don't fucking do it! You see what people do is send photos to the lover in the hopes that they will be for the eyes of their lover only. But here's the problem: people break up. People get mad. People become vindictive. What I have experienced people doing is saying okay, I'll let you take a picture of me but you have to delete it soon thereafter. Which in my opinion makes absolutely no sense and the reason why is because you have no proof that the individual you sent the picture to is actually going to destroy the picture that was sent. That's number one. Number two; almost every form of technology I have experienced has the capability to be compromised. This means if you delete something, it can be retrieved. So while you may be sitting there saying 'okay he or she deleted the photo of me sticking this into a place it has no business on earth being' he or she can go into the recently deleted section of the phone and pull that picture right the fuck back up and share it with the rest of the world. People do this because they are vengeful because of something the other may have done. People do this because they want to show that one special person that intimate times were shared between this person and the guy or girl of their dreams. People do this because...nevermind why they do this, just understand that people do things like this and more. And if you are in a relationship thinking that you can trust the person you are involved with to keep your sexy lingerie pics or inappropriate types of intimacy pics private, you may be in for a rude awakening. I tell people this all the time: you are not trusting another man or woman. You are attempting to trust the human spirit. The human spirit is not perfect. So what outcome could you possibly hope to expect when you already know nobody is infallible?

Just A Couple More Things About Cheating

When it comes to committing infidelity, there are two kinds of people smart and impulsive. When it comes to detecting infidelity, they are the same. An impulsive person will say 'gimmie your phone, who is this bitch?' 'Who is this motherfucker?' This person is a hothead and will make the life of the other in the relationship an unnecessary hell, especially if that person is innocent. A smart person will plan for the possibility of infidelity. He or she will buy not one but two phones – one for him and one for her. He or she will have both phones on the same account so that he or she will have access to all calls, messages, and activity on that account. If the other already has a phone, then there is always the 'oops, I dropped your phone by accident and it is smashed beyond repair. Sorry honey. But because I love you so much I will buy you a new one.' And once the new one is bought, then go ahead with the plan above. A smart person, if unsure of a late night phone call or any call and the significant other will not show the phone, will not get mad and belligerent. The smart person will note the time at which the call is received; wait until the time is right and go through the phone. And when is the right time? Whenever the significant other goes to sleep. They will have to sleep sometime. You see what's expected is for the significant other to flip out over a situation they more than likely do not understand. You must be the smart and in control person in this scenario. Don't do what's expected, do what's smart. And unexpected. This will put the other in such a comfort zone that he or she will think that you do not care about the activities of the other. And if this person is doing you dirty, then it will not be that hard to catch them.

In regard to cheating, the one thing, which is mandatory for happiness or continued happiness, like everything else in this world, is follow your own rules. Do not live according to what others say about how your life and your life's interactions should go. If somebody cheats on you and you want to keep this person in your life then do so. Fuck those who say he or she will only do it again. Fuck those who say I got rid of my cheating ass husband or wife after one indiscretion. The relationship you have is your relationship. The life you have is your life. Tell motherfuckers to stay out of both because only then will you have true happiness. Now don't get me wrong because many people will take my words out of context and go and fuck up their already fucked up relationships even more. By following your own rules and doing your own thing, I do not mean for you to have no idea of any possible ramifications nor bother to learn any and then just do whatever comes naturally. No. That is a recipe for disaster. What I am saying is understand what will happen or what is likely going to happen if you respond in a certain manner or choose a certain course of action. Find out all of the possible outcomes from staying with this cheating motherfucker vs. getting rid of his or her lying ass. Then after you have all of this information, make an informed decision. What infidelity, along with the advice of nosey motherfuckers will have the average person doing is foregoing their own common sense and doing things, which are totally uncharacteristic of them. For instance, people become so attached to the significant other, so attached to the relationship, that if an indiscretion is committed, the significant other will not say you have done something, which was totally on your own, something, which is hurtful and detrimental to you, or something which deserves penance. No, the significant other will say you hurt me. The whole relationship will be based around that one act – but note the whole relationship is only based around that one act after the act of infidelity has been perpetrated. Before infidelity, everything is 50/50. You get your paycheck, the significant other is right there saying half of that shit is mine. You win the lottery with a ticket that you bought with your own money, the significant other is right there saying half of that shit is mine. But just let it be a situation of you taking your dick out and sticking it into another person and getting caught, the significant other will be right there saying 'no motherfucker, you did that shit all on your own!' And not only that, the significant other will desire revenge more than anything else. More than forgiveness, more than talking about it and working it out. Infidelity is probably the only thing in relationships, which is done, and is believed to be done to intentionally hurt the other party. A person can wake up in the middle of the night, slap the shit out of the significant other and say 'baby, I was having a nightmare, I didn't know what I was doing' and there will be a better chance of that being believed than a person 'accidentally' having an affair. People won't say 'well maybe you didn't know what you were doing.' People will be like 'no motherfucker, you knew exactly what you were doing!' You see, infidelity is always believed to be deliberate. There is never a thing of 'I was too drunk to be in control of my actions, or I was sleeping and I didn't know what I was doing' when it comes to infidelity. And because of this belief, many people feel that the best way of getting past the act of infidelity is to make the committing party share in the hurt that the innocent significant other may be feeling at that present point or all throughout the relationship. The healing process does not include 'we will get past this honey and we will be stronger as a couple after we get past this.' The healing process all too often includes 'oh yeah motherfucker, you wanna cheat on me? I got something for your ass. Watch this!' And with the 'watch this' people will go off on a

'I'm gonna get all of the dick or pussy I can' spree' just to show their male or female superiority. Many people who get cheated on will not cheat one time as revenge. They will cheat damn near til their dicks fall off or until the vaginas get so sore that they can't pee for a couple of days. You see, sex is the most important thing in a relationship to many, many people. Violating that vow is considered to be a crime, which can only be surpassed by murder. And you best believe that sometimes this violation can lead up to murder also. But you see, this is the exact reason people need to get to know who it is they are sleeping with.

One of the big reasons why infidelity causes breakups is because no matter what an individual says about the sex only lasting during the sex act and the feelings doing the same, people expect that the person they share intimacies with to be there during the lonely and unhappy times in their lives. They expect that when there is a thunderstorm and the sound of the thunder makes an individual cry and cling to the sheets for dear life, that the one he or she is sleeping with would be right there beside him or her to soothe those fears. But the thought of this person being with somebody else is what bitch slaps the other into the realization of you are second and you will always be second when it comes to the relationship of the other. And this is what people number one, do not like and number two, do not expect, until after it happens.

That is the time that these people who are 'second' begin to make that bid for first place. Then the people in the relationship, who thought that the sexual relationship was going to be just that are too bitch slapped by reality. They begin to realize 'hey wait a minute, this man or woman actually does have feelings for me, and may cause a problem between my significant other and I.' Then comes damage control mode. Then these people start lying and pretending that they actually care about the one who was just used for sex so that he or she does not become the 'fatal attraction' type stalker. These people spend much of their time focusing on the preventive maintenance, which should have been done ahead of time, and by doing so they are taking time away from the significant other at home. Now it goes without saying the significant other will most assuredly notice that the other is not focusing all of their attention at home and the most often thought will be that the other is 'distant.' This will lead to questions, which will lead to lies, which will lead to the covering of tracks, which will eventually lead to arguments about suspected infidelity.

Opposite Sex Protocol

Whether people realize it or not, relationships are often about game play. They are about manipulation. They are about every type of strategic planning and execution imaginable. <u>They are about everything except love.</u> When it comes to making love – no wait, let's scrap all of that political correctness stuff. When it comes to having sex, there are many rules that are gender dependent. Guy code, girl code stuff. Now one of those, which is guy code is when relating to sexual positions, is that doggie style has to be the favorite. And why? It is because this position is the most male dominating position there is. It is the most emotionally disconnected position and on top of that, when in that position, guys can think of and fantasize being with any other woman in the world and the reason why is because they do not have to look at whom they are dominating. All they get to see is a backside. And that backside can belong to any woman they so choose. One of the things, which often falls under girl code, is 'the one who goes down first is the weakest' thing. You see the thing about having sex nowadays is not that it is a two partner, shared activity. It is not 'we had sex' or 'we made love.' Nowadays it is more 'I made that bitch suck my dick' or 'I made that motherfucker lick my pussy.' 'I made him or her submit to me.' Does this sound crass or inappropriate or like something you partner would never in a million years say? If you answered yes, well good. This is more than likely how the oh so sweet significant other talks when he or she is not with you. You see the major hypocrisy in the relationship world is that people think the side, which is shown by the significant other is the only side, which the significant other has to show. But you see, this is the expectation that we many times project onto the significant other. We expect him or her to always be as nice as they were the first day or week we met them. Now think for a second how much bullshit is actually contained within that last statement. I mean you have a mean streak sometimes don't you? Of course you do. Everybody does. And so does the significant other. We just never expect to see it or hear it or think that it exists. This is one of the major problems in relationships. You see with sex, it is almost a sin for a guy to make love or admit that he has made love to his woman. Can you imagine the backlash a man would receive if he were to hang out with the fellas and say 'my girl and I spent the weekend making love' as opposed to 'I fucked the shit out of that ass' or a woman saying 'he fucked the shit out of me!' The sad but true and necessary thing about relationships is that everything you need to hear is everything you will never hear. People will tell you what you want to hear all the time but need? That's something completely different. The reason there is so much deception in relationships is because the one thing we ask of the significant other, is the one thing they will never give. That thing is them showing us the offensive side. The hang out with their buddies or bff's side. The side where they talk about how much they really hate the opposite sex and would not even be bothered if it weren't for the necessity. People say I want to know everything about you but the other will never divulge and the simple reason why he or she will never divulge is because they can't. Nobody in this world can handle a person who is totally truthful. Total truth will never equal total happiness. One of the bigger myths about achieving total happiness in a relationship is the one about giving up your happiness so that your partner can be happy. This is what one can call a two sided sword. Now while I believe that no relationship is successful without at least minimal change on the part of both parties, a complete sacrificing of one's happiness is guaranteed travel toward detriment. The thing about sacrifice, which many in relationships do not completely understand, is that the amount of sacrifice must be chosen and distributed according to the level of comfort of each party.

Unhealthy Relationship Speech

One of the biggest problems that people have in relationships, which often stay dormant until people are two seconds away from choking the life out of their significant other is the thing of putting up with shit for too long. People put up with things that they do not like then when one gets tired of it and says something to the other, the other responds with well you do a lot of shit I don't like too. I just didn't say anything. This right here is both a communication issue and a deception issue. It is communication because people did not discuss what was making them unhappy at the prime moment for discussion. And that prime moment is when the shit first makes them unhappy. Not several weeks, months and or years later. It is also a deception issue because the two individuals in the relationship are giving each other and quite possibly the world at large the belief that they are happy and problem free. Now one of the biggest issues that is allowed to remain in a relationship without ever being spoken about is how people talk to one another. People in relationships have become the epitome of cartoon violence. You don't expect to see it. You don't realize that it is as prevalent as it is, but it's there. The thing about cartoon violence, which is closely related to the way people talk to one another is that with the violence in cartoons, most will downplay its existence. They will say it's harmless. They will assume the kids watching don't know any better. But they are wrong. Just like with the harsh and sometimes completely disrespectful way people in relationships talk to one another, many will say that it is normal for couples to settle into a comfort zone where talking to the significant other in what others could interpret as disrespectful is normal or commonplace. People will call the significant other names like stupid, asshole, and worse. And the bad thing about this is the fact that people allow this to continue. You see, the home and more importantly who is in the home is supposed to be seen as a place of refuge. It is seen the same way a soft pillow is seen to someone who wants nothing more in this world than to rest the head onto that pillow and sleep for about 36 hours straight. I think that we are all in agreement when I say that nobody wants to come home to a piece of concrete encased in a satin pillowcase. And this is all too often how the significant other appears to the one needing comfort. The other looks appealing and welcoming but as soon as we get close enough to experience that welcome or comfort, then comes the uncomfortable feeling. You see nobody wants to sleep on a hard pillow but this is exactly how some in relationships present themselves to the significant other. This hard pillow type of existence makes the significant other not want to immediately come home. This hard pillow type of existence makes the significant other not want to move in or live together with the significant other. And this is one of the things that many in relationships do not understand. People are too often under the impression that if they do everything, which is expected or is done by most of society, then the other will not only have no choice but to accept the relationship, he or she will overlook any type of adversity which is considered not that extreme. They will say things to the effect of I'm a woman. It's my job to be a bitch, and the man is just supposed to handle it. Or they will be under the impression that sometimes men get on their period and the woman should just wait it out or ignore the man until he comes around to acting what they interpret as normal. You see, this is accepted behavior, but it is not liked behavior. And yes, there is a difference. When people put up with things for the sole purpose of peace in the relationship, these things often have a way of later resurfacing and causing more drama later on down the line. It's just like when a relationship is initiated and people ignore the fact that the other smokes, when they don't smoke themselves or don't like those who smoke but they become involved in a relationship regardless. Then months or years down the line when whatever initial attraction, which was had, fades away and the true feeling about the habits of the significant other is revealed, the relationship will hit that relationship ending fork in the road. This is what happens when people keep putting up with things just for peace and quiet in their relationships. Sooner or later one will get tired of coming home to an attitude. Sooner or later one will get tired of coming home to letting you say whatever you want just because he or she does not feel like arguing with someone who does not quit or more importantly does not understand the perspective of the significant other. This is why complete honesty and adversity in the beginning of relationships is absolutely necessary for the relationship's continuance. Sure it would be nice if everybody could go through a relationship without ever having an argument, but since that is never going to happen, the next best course of action is to get to know each other as much as possible before getting into something based on lies and pacification. If more people were completely honest and said 'I do not like the way you talk to me' and they said this each and every time the significant other talked in a way, which was unfavorable or unwelcome, then sooner, rather than later, the other would learn what not to do in the relationship which was not acceptable to the first. But people just wanna say 'alright, I'll let it go this time' not realizing that letting it go this time, is just making the foundation that much more comfortable for a next time, and a next time and a next time. The really bad thing about the putting up with shit for too long thing is that we all know how to easily fix it. How? Stop putting up with shit you do not like. If

336

your significant other curses at you or calls you out of your name in a playful manner, then tell him or her that that is something that you do not approve of. If he or she says that you are too serious, then you respond with 'you damned right! Now don't do it again.' Once people have a clear understanding of what you do not like, then there will be less chance of them doing it to you. If they continue to do what you do not like, then leave their retarded asses. Simple. I know what so many of you are thinking. You are thinking that relationships are supposed to be all 'I love you this' and 'I love you that' and whatever there is that I may not love about you, it's okay because we will work through it so that we find a mutually agreeable solution. No. Relationships are only like that when, as stated elsewhere in this publication, you have the perfect couple and the perfect relationship. That will never happen. The unfortunate and unspoken part about relationships is that you will have to train, yes I said train your significant other to treating you how you want and expect to be treated. And believe it or not, this is one of the easiest things to do in a relationship. You see, once a person gets a clear understanding of how you will react to whatever it is they do or say, nine times out of ten, they will adjust their behavior accordingly. This is how people get trapped off in those emotional and physical prisons of 'he always curses at me' or 'she won't let me do this.' Think about this on a criminal level:

why is it there are so many repeat offenders? It's because the punishment is too easy. If everybody, not just a certain race of people, were subject to the harshest penalties for even the simplest of crimes, they would not commit the crime. (Unless of course there were mental issues involved.) The thing that people do not want to accept is that every relationship out here, unless it is one, which is forced through arranged marriages or the pimp / hoe methodology, is a choice. You choose to deal with the asshole or retarded bitch you are presently dealing with. The difference is they never seem like the asshole or retarded bitch when you first get involved. What happens is that over time, they change their behavior. This is problem number one. Then what happens is over time, is you choose to accept that change in their behavior. This is problem number two.

When you go to the supermarket and shop for groceries, do you fill your cart up with anything you do not like? Of course not. And why? It's because you do not like the shit you don't like. You are investing your money, so why would you waste money on something you are not going to enjoy? The same thinking has to be applied to relationships. The only difference is that you are investing your time. If there is something, which tries to get into the shopping cart of your life, then pretend you are at the store and put that shit back on the shelf or better yet, don't even allow it into your cart. Don't even pick that shit up.

Now this is not to be confused with believing that the fear of not wanting to make the significant other mad, is actually the only way they can be made happy. People cause this fear by not having reasonable conversations about the other not living up to the expectations, which are had in the relationship but by arguing and complaining and generally pissing the other the fuck off. And proof of this is how many people will say things to the effect of 'no, I can't hang out, I don't wanna hear my wife's mouth' or 'I gotta wash the dishes so she doesn't whine and complain' or 'I have to act this way because I know how he or she gets.' To me, this is not the meaning behind a happy relationship. This is my emotions and responses are controlling how you exist in this relationship. A relationship should be 'hey, this is how I am. If you accept me how I am, there should be no need for me to change, unless I want to. And if I decide to change, then the only reason will be because I want to make you happier than you were when you accepted me.' You see, people outside of the relationship will say things to the effect of 'you're scared of your wife' or 'you're letting your man rule you.' That is not always the case. This is not being scared of the significant other, as much as it is knowing which boundaries are to be respected and not crossed.

The best relationships in the world, in my opinion at least, are the ones where I do everything that you like and you do the same for me. Since we know that this is hovering near the category of perfection, whatever a person does that the other does not like, either tweak it ever so much that it is tolerable or as stated above, leave that retarded mf. You can always find a new significant other. It's the peace of mind, which is many times elusive.

This brings to close yet another edition from highly controversial author Jeremiah Dotson. Opinions and comments always welcome facebook.com/superauthor Jeremiah Dotson. Until next time and oh yes, there will be a next time.